Point Pleasant Park

Point Pleasant Park

An Illustrated History

Janet Kitz and Gary Castle

Pleasant Point Publishing

Pleasant Point Publishing
PO Box 758
Halifax NS B3J 2V2
e-mail: image@fox.nstn.ca

Editing: Paula Sarson
Design: Nancy Roberts
Cover photos: Gary Castle
Scanning: Jim Clark
Layout, pp. 170-172: Gary Castle
Printed and bound by: Transcontinental Printing

Canadian Cataloguing in Publication Data

    Kitz, Janet F., 1930-

        Point Pleasant Park

        ISBN 0-9686308-0-4

    1. Point Pleasant Park (Halifax, N.S.) -- History.   2. Halifax (N.S.) -- History.
    I. Castle, Gary, 1948-   II. Title.

    FC2346.65.P65K58 1999   971.6'225   C99-950247-6
    F1039.5.H17K58 1999

To all the Park users,
past, present and future

LIST OF THE SETTLERS WHO CAME OUT WITH GOVERNOR CORNWALLIS TO CHEBUCTO, IN JUNE 1749.

(COPY.)

The original Mess Book of the Settlers, of which this is a copy, was deposited in the office of the Registrar of the Court of Vice Admiralty, at Halifax, but has been missing for several years. Letters opposite names of Settlers refer to Notes at end of this list.

SHIP CHARLTON Frigate, *Richard Ladd, Master, Burthen 395 Tons,* 197.

Names.	Quality.	Children		Servants		Total.	Regiment, Ship, &c.
		Males.	Females.	Males.	Females.		
Alexander Hay & wife	Surgeon's Mate	1	1	..	..	4	Revenge.
Thos. Henry Willoughby & wife	Millwright	..	..	..	1	3	
Edwd. Pomfret and wife	Patternmaker	..	..	..	1	3	Prince of Orange.
Willm. Whiteacre	Mariner	..	..	..	..	1	Bellona.
Thomas Gifford and wife	Mariner	1	..	..	..	3	Anson.
Wm. Cannon & wife	Mariner	..	..	..	..	2	Solebay.
Edwd. Stokes & wife	Mariner	1	2	..	..	5	Princessa.
John Hart and wife	Mariner	..	..	..	..	2	
Willm. Giles & wife	Taylor	..	..	..	..	2	
Willm. Hall & wife	Taylor	..	2	..	..	4	
Peter Hart	Smith	..	..	..	..	1	
John Duncan & wife	Mariner	..	1	..	..	3	Royal George.
Thos. Gore & wife	Private man	..	..	..	1	3	Royal Irish.
John Burnside	Volunteer	..	..	1	..	2	Capn. Morrice's Coy.
Thos. Burnside	Midshipman	..	..	1	..	2	Hector.
Stirker Nelson & wife	Mariner	..	..	..	..	2	Monmouth.
Thos. Waldegrave & wife	Private man	1	..	..	..	3	1st Regt. Foot Gds.
Jas. Spratt	Private	..	..	..	..	1	Paulet's.
Thos. Drury	Mariner	..	..	..	1	2	Tavistock.
Robert Hilton	Mariner	..	..	..	..	1	La Fore's.
Wm. Costring	Smith	..	..	..	..	1	
Richd. Jackson	Perriwigmaker	..	..	2	..	3	
Alexr. Ross	Husbandman	..	..	..	..	1	
Anthy. Castle and wife	Smith	1	..	..	..	3	
Saml. Bradshaw and wife	Cooper	..	..	..	..	2	
Thos. Davis & wife	Braizer	..	..	..	..	2	
Philip Landerback and wife	Taylor	1	1	..	..	4	
Gotlieb Shermiller and wife	Butcher	1	..	1	..	4	
Christian Trider and wife	Husbandman	2	2	..	..	6	
Jason Chapman	Private	..	..	..	..	1	Bowle's.
Willm. Howsman and wife	Husbandman	..	..	..	1	3	
Richd. Jones	Turner	..	..	..	..	1	
Alexr. Clarke	Shipwright	..	..	..	..	1	
Morrice Grant & wife	Bricklayer	..	..	2	..	4	
John Povery & wife	Boatman	..	..	..	1	3	
Thomas Temple & wife	Husbandman	..	1	..	..	3	
Robert Ewer	Lieutenant	..	..	3	2	6	Frazer's.
Stephen Hill & wife	Mariner	..	..	1	..	3	Tilbury.

Part of the list of people who came to Chebucto (Halifax) with Governor Cornwallis in 1749.

Some of these people began clearing the land at Pleasant Point and gave the area its name.

(Cambridge Military Library)

Contents

Photo Captions Key

Castle	Gary Castle
Citadel	Parks Canada, Citadel National Historic Site
Kitz	Janet Kitz
MCM	Maritime Command Museum
NSM	Nova Scotia Museum
P. P. P.	Point Pleasant Park Collection
P. P. P. Records	Point Pleasant Park Commission Records
PANS	Public Archives of Nova Scotia

All other images appear courtesy of other individuals or institutions named in parentheses at the end of captions throughout the book.

We apologize for the quality of certain reproductions. In order to include material that seemed important to the subject matter, poorer images were used if better ones proved unobtainable.

Preface

Very soon after my arrival in Halifax twenty-eight years ago I had my first walk in Point Pleasant Park. My immediate impression was that this place would make a difference to my life in Nova Scotia. How right I was.

Before many weeks had passed my daily routine included a visit to the Park. I became familiar with every path, the different views, and learned how to vary the route according to the weather. It took only a short time to get to know the park staff as they went about their duties, and to see how the Park was run.

Eventually I was asked to join the Point Pleasant Park Commission.

Three years ago, Gary Castle called me to ask if I would be interested in working on a book on Point Pleasant Park. He had been taking photographs there for thirty years, and was also interested in reproducing earlier works. Ever since I had been involved in the Park, I had been collecting bits and pieces concerning its history. We agreed to try to put our collections together, and that he would reproduce old photographs, maps and plans, while I would do the research and writing. At that time we had little idea of how much work it was going to involve, nor how many places it would take us.

For some of the Park features pictorial evidence is plentiful. From about 1870 to 1885, for example, the Royal Engineers photographed all the forts in the area, showing various angles and views. Other periods of time and sections of the Park caused much more difficulty. Hence certain chapters of the book are heavily illustrated, and others less so.

Park minutes, I believed, would give me most of the information I sought. That was true to some extent, but one problem arose. The first minute book had been lost. Letters in the early twenties complain about its disappearance. Scraps of minutes survived in the City

Hall records, and newspapers supplied some information on Commission meetings and decisions. Telephone calls to the businesses and families of Park Commissioners of the period yielded no information on the possible whereabouts of the book. I do not wish to preempt material that will appear later in this book, but some of the difficulties involved going through, frequently on rather poor microfilm, years of newspapers, and still coming up with no real solution to certain problems. Perhaps someone will read of the Sterns affair and the Montague Cup and solve the mysteries on which I have spent a great deal of fruitless effort.

The park lodge is a replica of the gatehouse at Disraeli's estate in England. That information I found in an isolated document. But why?

Disraeli died in 1848, years before the Park came into being. Had a commissioner visited England and thought that the gatehouse at Hughenden Manor would make an ideal park lodge? Diana Dalton, who chairs the Park Advisory Committee, brought me the guide book to the Manor, now a National Trust property. She saw resemblances in style here and there on the estate, but I stil do not know why that particular cottage was copied. The original gatehouse in England was torn down.

So the research has not been entirely straightforward. People have helped. When I have visited the Public Archives of Nova Scotia, made requests at museums, libraries and other sources, the interest and time-consuming detective work that has been carried out, though it may not always have produced the desired results, has been of great encouragement and stimulus.

Point Pleasant Park is a wonderful place. Anyone who has not walked there early on a September morning and watched the brilliant dawn spread over the ocean, with herons silhouetted like statues on the rocks, gulls made pink by the rising sun, cormorants with their wings spread out to dry, seals basking on the Hen and Chickens rocks, a tug going out to meet an arriving cruise ship, a great container ship leaving port, and the friendly people on their daily walk or run, has not experienced the very best that Halifax has to offer.

Janet Kitz

In the early 1960s I began photographing Point Pleasant Park. At that time, my interest was purely for pictorial purposes. I would spend entire days there. Gradually, I began to realize I was seeing this Park in a totally different way. I sensed that it had much more to offer, if only one took a closer look. I began not only to see the Park but to *feel* it.

If you enter Point Pleasant Park just before dusk on a foggy day and sit quietly in the forest, you can feel its soul. It will envelop you, and you will never forget the sensation. You will be compelled to return again and again. That's the magic of Point Pleasant Park.

Gary Castle

1

Pleasant Point
and Its Fortifications

On June 21, 1749, Colonel the Honourable Edward Cornwallis, recently named governor of Nova Scotia, arrived at Chebucto, escorting well over four thousand settlers for the colony. Before sending his first dispatch to London on June 22, 1749, he waited a day to permit exploration of this largely unknown territory for which he would be responsible. Giving experienced men one day to reconnoitre would at least provide useful first impressions. That report stated that the harbour was full of fish and was the finest his officers had ever seen. The country was "one continued wood," with not a clearing anywhere.

Ten days later, Sandwich Point—the name soon optimistically changed to Pleasant Point—was chosen as the site for the new settlement. The land had the fine harbour on one side and the Sandwich or Hawk's River on the

First impressions of Pleasant Point (PANS)

Colonel the Honourable Edward Cornwallis, first governor of Nova Scotia (PANS)

Halifax from Point Pleasant. South aspect of Halifax, Nova Scotia, 1789 by Lt. Col. E. Hicks. (PANS)

other. Later the "river" was discovered to be an arm of the sea and was given its more accurate name, Northwest Arm. All able-bodied men were ordered to fell trees and clear land.

In a short time, however, work stopped as serious disadvantages to the site were revealed. The first drawback was that the water on the ocean side lacked depth, allowing only small boats to anchor. Then, when weather conditions must have changed dramatically, it became painfully obvious that the location was too exposed to southeast gales. The site was abandoned for a more suitable one further up the harbour, from which the present-day City of Halifax has grown.

Two months after relocating the settlement, when defence was being planned, Pleasant Point was one of the three chosen sites. (The high land opposite, later called York Redoubt, and George's Island were the others.) Settlers were quickly organized to form a militia. On Sunday, December 10, 1749, after divine service, all males between the ages of sixteen and sixty were ordered to provide themselves with weapons and ammunition and to work on fortifications. Neglect or refusal of duty would result in twenty-four-hour imprisonment or a five-shilling fine.

In July 1758, a group of seamen walking beneath the pines at Pleasant Point was attacked by Mi'kmaq, who carried away two of the men and killed and scalped two more, possibly for their tarred pigtails—the common hairstyle for sailors at the time. After this incident, the point was patrolled by armed soldiers. The Mi'kmaq chief disappeared, and it was believed that he had been killed by some of the soldiers. Legend has it that he was secretly buried in the woods of Pleasant Point.

It did not take long for a track to develop from the main part of the early town along the harbour to Pleasant Point. The route, known as Pleasant Street, had become a popular walk for the early settlers on a fine Sunday, the only day of rest for most. After the incident between the Mi'kmaq and the seamen, the military provided patrols, and the armed redcoats gave the citizens enough confidence to enjoy their strolls.

On Saturday, July 12, 1762, fear of a French invasion prompted a Council of War held at the governor's house in Halifax. Present were: "The Honble Jona. Belcher, Esqr., Lieut. Govr. of Nova Scotia, The right Honble lord Colvill as commander in Chief of His Majesty's Ships in North America, Colonl. Richard Bulkely of the Halifax Militia, Major Genl. Bastide, Colo. Wm. Forster, Lt. Colo. Hamilton, Lt. Colo. Winslow."* The sixth resolution stated: "It having been proposed to the board that a battery or batteries should be erected at point Pleasant, the same was agreed to, and resolved that Major Genl. Bastide should give such directions therein as he may judge the most expedient ..."

Two days later the group continued its Council of War. Minutes of the previous meeting were read, approved and signed. It was further resolved, among other measures, that "a detachment of a Captain, Three Subalterns, four Sergeants, four Corporals & a Hundred Privates of the Provincials be ordered and March to Morrow Morning, and encamp at Pleasant point on the spot that shall be directed by the Engineers attending; in order to erect a Battery of Ten Nine-pounders agreeable to the resolution of the 10th Instant."

Three days later at a continuation of the Council of War, Lord Colvill "acquainted the Council of War in writing" that he had placed the only warship available at a strategic point for defence until batteries should be completed. The

*Taken from papers relating to the First Settlement of Halifax, 1749–1756. Published under a resolution of the House of Assembly passed March 15, 1865. Edited by Thomas B. Atkins, D.C.L. Cambridge Library.)

OLD FRENCH FORT HALIFAX. Showing bolt used to Chain the Harbour.

HALIFAX SKETCH.—BY OUR SPECIAL ARTIST.

The remains of Chain Rock Battery are visible 1991. (Castle)

Halifax sketch from *Canadian Illustrated News,* August 13, 1881. Note the inaccurate caption on the sketch. The fort was British. The chain crossed the Northwest Arm. (PANS)

ship could be moved to any position where her guns were needed. He also stated that he was making "a Boom of Timber and Iron Chains of 120 fathom long to Run across the North West arm." It was resolved that "to Support and protect the Boom … two Sloops of the Largest Size that can be found, be immediately taken into the Service and properly manned and Armed." At a meeting on July 23, 1762, Major General Bastide reported that all these plans had been carried out.

Two batteries were in place as protection from attack by sea. These came to be known as North West Arm, later called Flagstaff, Battery and Point Pleasant or Fielding's Battery on the shore facing the

Atlantic. These defences were of necessity hastily thrown up and of a temporary nature. Reinforcement and repair had to be undertaken with every new threat of attack from the sea. Also, three cannon were mounted on the higher ground, pointing out over the boom across the Northwest Arm, which was secured to an iron ring fixed into the bedrock. (The name of the nearby modern street is Chain Rock Drive.)

The American Revolution in 1776 brought discontent with British rule too close for complacency and, by 1778, the Black Rock Battery and Chain Battery had been added to strengthen the fortifications. A simple fort, mainly earthworks, the Chain Rock Battery was constructed

on the Arm side of Pleasant Point, just above the rock where the ring for the chain was embedded, although the boom itself was no longer in use. In 1796, a new boom was built but lasted only a short time. Chain Rock Battery was abandoned about 1800.

By 1790, the defences had fallen into sorry state. Early in 1793, when war broke out between Britain and France, attack by the French fleet was feared. A flurry of activity erupted. The harbour defences were strengthened and given additions. John Wentworth, appointed governor of Nova Scotia the previous year, raised a provincial regiment of militia to protect the city. By 1794, ninety-five militia members were employed in fort repairs. The general in command of the Halifax garrison ordered the construction of a new fort in the woods at Point Pleasant. To it his own name was

Sir John Wentworth, Bart. Born at Portsmouth, N. H., 1737; died at Halifax, 1820. Lieutenant-Governor of Nova Scotia, 1792–1808. (Citadel)

Above and below, Fort Ogilvie between 1870 and 1875 (PANS also NSM)

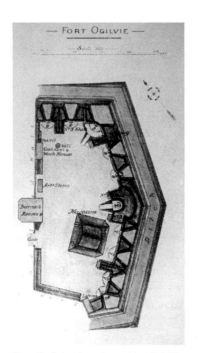

Fort Ogilvie plan signed by J. Millar, Lt. R. E., 1863 (Citadel)

Fort Ogilvie, Royal Engineers, 1870–1885 (NSM)

Fort Ogilvie 1998 (Castle)

given, Fort Ogilvie. The battery was a half-moon shape, faced with sod, with six 24-pounders mounted on traversing platforms facing the harbour. In the rear was built a guardhouse and included at the site was a furnace for heating shot.

A year later, soldier son of George III, Prince Edward, Duke of Kent, arrived in Halifax, replacing General Ogilvie as military commander-in-chief of Nova Scotia. Fortification intensified with Prince Edward's zeal and disregard for expense.

Prince Edward ordered the construction of three towers for the defence of Halifax in 1796. Two years earlier, at Cape Mortella on Corsica, in the Mediterranean, the might of a British military expedition had been thwarted by a low, seemingly insignificant tower manned by a relatively small number of soldiers. The tower, which held for an incredible length of time against all-out attack, was round, with extremely thick walls and only one entrance some twenty feet above the ground. Towers of a similar type, named Martello Towers—a slight variation on the name of the cape—were built on various parts of the British coastline against French attack towards the end of the century.

Whether Prince Edward was influenced by the tower at Cape Mortella is not certain; however, he was reputedly fond of round structures. The first, at Point Pleasant, was named the Prince of Wales Tower, for Prince Edward's older brother, the future king. Funds for its construction were originally refused, although work had begun in 1796. Edward overcame the opposition, insisting that French attack was imminent and that, although the area was supplied with coastal defences, it was vulnerable to a land invasion. By 1798, the strongest Point Pleasant fortification was completed. Working parties from the Royal Nova Scotia Regiment were paid for their labour.

Although the Prince of Wales Tower is round, with a thick stone wall, it is not of exactly the same

Prince Edward, Duke of Kent (Citadel)

design as the Corsican tower, whose height and diameter measured more or less the same, and originally it was not called a Martello Tower. The Prince of Wales Tower is nearly three times as wide as it is high, has a hollow central pillar rather than a solid one, and, in the beginning, had a wooden roof instead of stone.

The tower, on its high ground, commanded an imposing area. It gave cover to Fort Ogilvie, Point Pleasant and the North West Arm Batteries and was designed to control passage through the Northwest Arm. To allow the defenders a view of enemy ships approaching, all trees south of the tower were removed.

The Prince of Wales Tower helped to make the whole area impregnable. Six guns pointed threateningly through embrasures in the roof, and

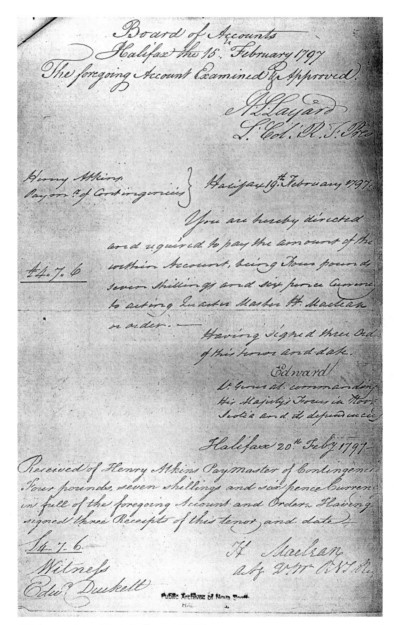

Bill for work on Martello Tower (PANS)

Halifax Nova Scotia

Pay list of Working Parties, &c.ca of the Royal Nova Scotia Regiments, employed on the New Tower, building at Point Pleasant, under the Direction of Lieut. William Fenwick, Commanding Royal Engineer By Order of Lieut. General his Royal Highness Prince Edward, between the 25th Novemr. & 24 Decemr. 1796, inclusive, Amounting in the whole to the Sum of Four Pounds, Seven Shillings & Sixpence —

W Fenwick Lieut.
Comm.g Royl Engineer

When Employed	Rank	No. of days	Pay Per day	Halifax Currency		
				£	s	d
New Tower	Artificers	52	1/3	3	5	
Point Pleasant	Rank & File	30	19d	1	2	6
				4	7	6

Certified —
Wentworth Col.

H Maclean
Asst. D Mr. R N S. Regt.

PUBLIC Archives of Nova Scotia
HALIFAX, N.S.

Halifax Nova Scotia the 10th February 1797 Examined and Approved, for Four Pounds seven shillings and sixpence currency —

Jacob Heurd Junr.
Actg Compr. of Army Accts.

Second page of bill for work on Martello Tower (PANS)

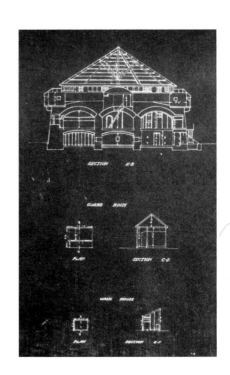

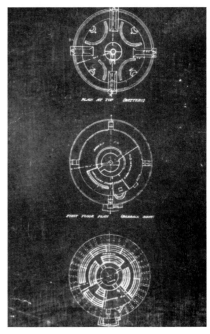

Plans for the Martello Tower (Citadel)

VIEW AT STATION "R".

VIEW AT STATION "S".

Views of the Martello Tower (Citadel) and an outbuilding

Martello Tower, Halifax, N. S.

Additions to the tower (Kitz)

four more aimed from the top storey. The ground floor was intended as a storeroom, or magazine, and the shaft in the centre allowed ammunition to be hoisted to the gunners above. The upper floor was designed to house about two hundred men but was usually manned by much fewer. Two fireplaces had been built into the wall to provide some comfort for the resident troops. However, the wooden roof was useless. It furnished little or no protection against rain and snow and was unable to take the weight of its own defensive guns. In any case, as the gunpowder was frequently soaked, their firing ability had proved unreliable in practice sessions.

Against enemy attack the tower's effectiveness could only be surmised, as, fortunately, it was never put to the test. It quickly became unserviceable, until an arched roof was built in 1811, more than ten years after Prince Edward had left Halifax. The new roof allowed eight guns to be mounted there, two more than previously. A brick magazine for storing ammunition so that it remained dry had been added to the ground floor, as well as an entrance. By then the name "Martello Tower"—more accurate since the fortification was closer to the standards that had been approved for the British towers in 1804—came into general use.

In the 1812 inspectional report, the North West Arm Battery was described as low and well situated to prevent an enemy from passing up the Northwest Arm. It was enclosed on the land side by a picket fence, had a furnace for heating shot and three English 18-pounders mounted on iron carriages. Four 24-pounders were to be mounted immediately. The battery was in good order, with one hundred rounds of ammunition prepared for each piece of ordnance.

On March 14, 1840, the ground beside the Martello Tower made the ideal setting for a drama. John Halliburton, the lawyer son of Chief Justice Halliburton, took offence at a derogatory reference to his father in

The site of Howe's duel is pictured on this souvenir vase. (Kitz)

Above, North West Arm Battery (PANS)

Below, the view out to sea from where the North West Arm Battery stood. (Castle)

one of Joseph Howe's speeches. Halliburton challenged Howe to a duel. Pistols for two at dawn! As duelling rules demanded, two friends tried to dissuade the combatants, but Halliburton was adamant. Honour had to be satisfied.

The two chosen friends stood in the middle of the clearing, back to back, acting as the duellists' seconds. Slowly, deliberately, they paced off the distance, then stood aside, giving place to the contenders. Facing each other, pistols at the ready, they awaited the drop of the handkerchief that signalled "Fire!"

Halliburton's bullet narrowly missed his opponent, but Howe, a dead shot, fired into the air. "I will not deprive an aging father of his son," he is reputed to have said. There was no reloading. Honour was satisfied. Howe had left four letters in case of his death: to his wife, to the people of Nova Scotia, and two dealing with business matters.

In 1862, the tower was converted for use as a fortified magazine to supply the other Point Pleasant batteries. Concrete and brick strengthened floors and roofs. The lower storey was divided into three parts, one with storage racks for

The Martello Tower's conversions (Castle). To the left is the roof, showing three of the four gun platforms and the roofed central column.

1,250 barrels of gunpowder, the others to make it ready for use. The second-storey door was cut into the barrack room level, and outside steps were built. Four machicolated galleries were added to the top of the structure to enable soldiers to supply flanking fire and protect the building. A small guard was mounted there at all times. The barrack room housed NCOs and eighteen men, but, in the event of attack, it could hold up to a hundred. The other area of the upper level was used as a small arms store. By 1865, the artillery on the roof had been reduced to four 32-pounders on traversing platforms.

The Halifax First Militia Brigade continued to enroll men, keeping the force trained and on an active service footing. A duty of fourpence a gallon was levied on the import of rum to pay for militia expenses.

Earlier, about 1805, when the outer area of Point Pleasant Battery had slid into the sea from the constant erosion of the waves, a more permanent rebuilding took place. An 1812 military report on Point Pleasant Battery states:

This Battery is well Situated on a low Point of Land, near the Water's edge with Rocks extending a Considerable

Above, Martello Tower 1995 (Castle)

Below, Point Pleasant Battery plan January 19, 1906 (PANS)

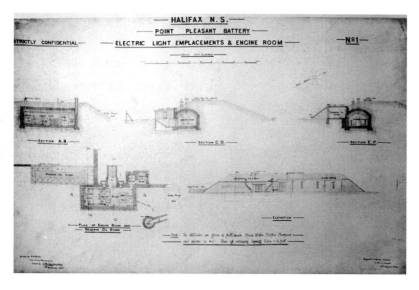

HALIFAX N.S.
POINT PLEASANT BATTERY
STRICTLY CONFIDENTIAL — ELECTRIC LIGHT EMPLACEMENTS & ENGINE ROOM — N°1

distance into the Harbour in its front, its Rear is enclosed with a Picket fence.

It has a Furnace for heating shot. The object of this work is to dispute a passage up the North West [sic] Arm as well as the Entrance of the Harbour.

It is faced with sod and is in good repair.

Mounted in the battery were six 24-pounders on traversing platforms and one 12-Pounder on an iron carriage. One hundred rounds of ammunition were available for each gun, some in travelling magazines on the battery, and the rest were stored in the stone magazine or storeroom. There was also a barrack and guardroom. The Point Pleasant Battery

occupied a considerable area of the shore.

According to the 1812 report, all forts, which normally housed only a small number of soldiers, were, in case of attack, "to be Manned by Volunteer Artillery, Inhabitants from the Town, and a few Royal Artillery."

By 1834, when no threat had appeared for several years, the Point Pleasant defences suffered from neglect. Only Point Pleasant Battery still contained armament— one 12-pounder.

The whole defence system became obsolete as new, longer range, more powerful guns were developed in the mid-1800s. An inspectional report was sent to the authorities in London, laying out the sad state of Halifax fortifications. In 1855, the commanding officer wrote that the city was in a "wholly unprotected condition." A flurry of activity took place that year when the 76th Artillery Regiment was encamped in the Park. Copies of a book (printed by Richard Nugent,

Guns from Point Pleasant Battery and interior of northeastern part circa 1880 (PANS)

Point Pleasant Battery August 6, 1942 (PANS)

Modern view of Point Pleasant Battery (Castle)

Arcade Building, Hollis Street, Halifax) from this period still exist. Interesting observations follow from *Hints on Bivouac and Camp Life* "issued by the Authority of His Excellency Major General Sir Gaspard Le Marchant for the guidance of Young Officers in the Garrison while under canvas for the summer months at the N W Arm Point Pleasant by Captain Wilford Brett, 76th Regiment, Aide de Camp. 1855."

The men were to depend entirely on themselves for daily necessities. They were, for example, to bake their own bread and kill their own meat "altogether unassisted by contractors or any class of citizens whatever." (According to an article on Chebucto, just then being explored by the British, in The London Magazine of 1749, "Woods abound with a variety of game, especially partridges which perch upon the trees and suffer themselves to be shot as often as you please." Even after a hundred

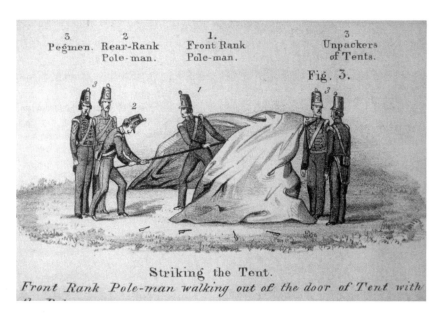

3. Pegmen. 2. Rear-Rank Pole-man. 1. Front Rank Pole-man. 3. Unpackers of Tents.

Fig. 3.

Striking the Tent.
Front Rank Pole-man walking out of the door of Tent with

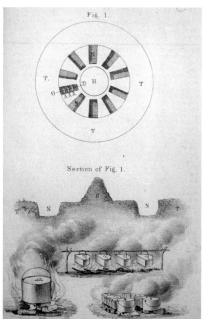

Fig. 1.

Section of Fig. 1.

years of European settlement, game may still have been fairly plentiful.)

The soldiers were to be given no materials. Ovens could be made from stones cemented with earth. After proper instruction the formation of a camp should require no more than three and a half minutes, the striking of it two and a half. Topics in the book include military manoeuvres, encamping, cooking in the field, baking, abbattoir, latrines, duties, fords, passage of rivers, bridges and drill.

At about this time, relations with the United States were tense, adding urgency to the dire warnings. In 1861, work began to improve the defences. Fort Ogilvie was enlarged and strengthened so that its guns covered the main ship channel and the harbour

Instructive sketches and illustrations from *Hints on Bivouac and Camp Life* (Citadel).

entrance. The work took almost eight years.

The year 1862 was busy with military works. The pessimistic reports had been taken seriously. The air must have rung with the sound of hammers pounding on stone. On the same day that the work began on Fort Ogilvie—August 5, 1862—construction of a new battery commenced, with "massive masonry and concrete substructures and casements," according to a report on the development of modern ordnance. Cambridge Battery would be situated about halfway between the Prince of Wales Tower, which had four small galleries added at this time, and the old Northwest Arm batteries, finally abandoned in 1862, when the new forts were begun. Powerfully armed, the Cambridge guns would cover the

Plan for Cambridge Battery
1863 (Citadel)

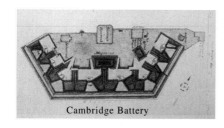

Cambridge Battery

Cambridge Battery
(Citadel)

Below, Cambridge
Battery (Col. R. W.
Chambers, PANS)

whole harbour entrance, including the opening to the Northwest Arm. Completed at the end of 1868, its total cost was £8,120, £2,000 less than the amount needed for the reconstruction of Fort Ogilvie. When heavier, more powerful guns were developed by 1873, the fort was adapted so they could be mounted.

In a little more than 120 years, the fortifications on Point Pleasant were built with great effort and expense. They were never called upon to fulfill their potential. Possibly, without their guardian presence, the feared attack from the sea might have become a reality.

Cambridge Battery
1998 (Castle)

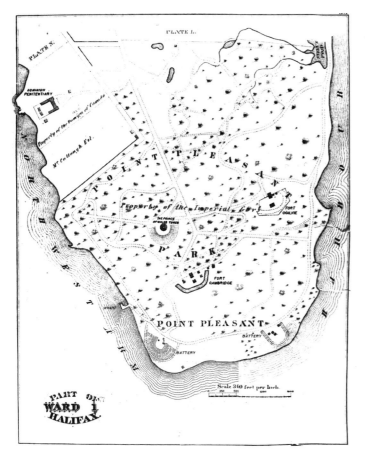

1879 map of
fortifications (Kitz)

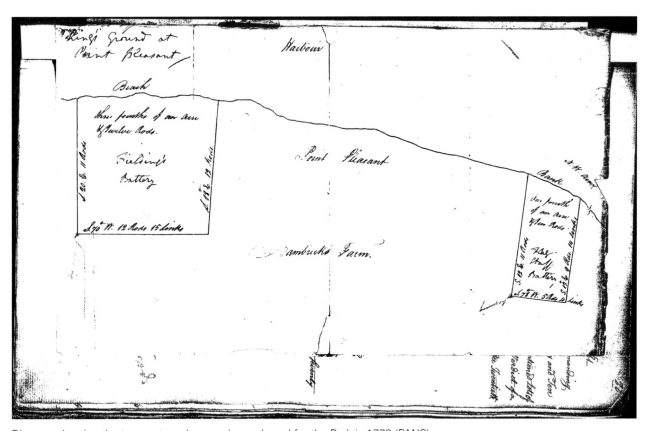

Diagram showing the two rectangular parcels purchased for the Park in 1778 (PANS)

2

The Park Lands

Province of Nova Scotia Halifax ss} Att His Majesty's Special Supreme Court held at Halifax on Fryday y[e] Twentieth Day of November in the Nineteenth Year of the Reign of the Lord George the Third, now King of Great Britain &c. and in the Year of Our Lord One Thousand Seven Hundred and Seventy Eight,

According to the force, form and Effect of a Certain Act made and Passed in the General Assembly of the Province Aforesaid in the Eighteenth Year of His Present Majesty's Reign, intitled an Act for the more speedy Settling the Value of such Lands as are or shall be Wanting to Erect Fortifications, or other Military Uses, Upon the Memorial of Hugh Bambrick of Halifax in the Province Aforesaid Yeoman

Original document (PANS)

... A jury of townsmen, all "good and lawfull men freeholders," met to assess a fair amount to be paid to Hugh Bambrick for two parcels of his land, one three-quarters of an acre and twelve roods, the other one-fourth of an acre and ten roods as shown on the map opposite.

Troops here, had been, and are made use of to erect fortifications, or other military uses, a certain Jury to wit. William Allen Esq.: Foreman, George Bayer, Baker, Richard Jacob, Baker, William Mott, Trader, John Hoccin jun.r Truckman, John Cleveland, Trader, Edmund Phelon, Innholder, John Jones, Sailmaker, Peter Mc. Nab, Cordwainer, Francis Boyd, Merchant, Andrew Cuenod, Merchant, John Willis, Innholder, John Kerby, Merchant, Alexander Ross, Carpenter, James Creighton, Truckman, William Boyle, Trader, John Fillis, Merchant, John Murphy, Innholder, Thomas Wagner, Butcher, Richard Cleary, Butcher, John William Schwartz, Merchant and Samuel Abro, Butcher, good and lawfull Men Freeholders, within the County aforesaid and residing in the Town of Halifax aforesaid, being summoned, called, impannelled and sworn, to &c.

These men were merchants, three innholders, truckmen, a cordwainer, two butchers and a sailmaker, among others. The sum "One hundred and Seventy-seven Pounds Thirteen Shillings and Ten Pence Nova Scotia Currency" was judged appropriate. On December 31, 1778, that amount was paid by W. Spry, Commanding Engineer.

Hugh Bambrick farmed the other, larger part of his Point Pleasant land. For many years traces of cultivation could be seen. That acreage was bought by General, later Lieutenant-Governor, Fanning about 1770. Here, opposite Purcell's Cove, he built a fine house surrounded by gardens. After living there only a few years, he sold the land to the Crown for £550. For some time the house was used by officers attached to the Point Pleasant forts. Later, Prince of Wales wharf was built below the house, opposite Purcell's Cove, and used for landing supplies and transferring troops.

On September 10, 1797, a letter was written to the Honourable Jonathan Sterns, former solicitor general of Nova Scotia, in respect to the sale of his land to the Crown.

Sir:

I have the honour of laying before his Royal Highness, Prince Edward, your letter of yesterday, relative to the sale of Point Pleasant, for four hundred pounds currency, of the Province, and have in command to acquaint you with his Royal Highness' acquiescence to your demand, as also your reservation of twenty-five acres as the North West part of said land.

I will thank you to inform me if it will answer your purpose to receive the four hundred pounds by quarterly payments of one hundred pounds each, the first payment to be made on the twenty-fourth instant.

I have the honour to remain,

Your most obedient, humble servant,
(Sgd.) Frederick Augustus Wetherall.

Before the agreement was signed, Jonathan Sterns died. His widow, with her advisers, the guardians of her children appointed in his will, went ahead with the negotiations to "sell and convey to His Majesty George the Third, the now King of Great Britain, etc. the lands and premises herein after described."

On September 17, 1798, Governor John Wentworth wrote Prince Edward, informing him, with "the utmost deference," that he had

attentively considered the deed of conveyance of the late Mr Sterns' property at Point Pleasant, purchased of him at a certain agreed price for Military purposes by your Royal Highness' Command, and possession then taken in behalf of the Crown, and on the same fortifications have been erected of great cost and importance, being fully of the opinion that the conveyance and security in the said Deed is perfectly safe and ample to Government.

I have the honour, herewith, to present it together with the account which they pray your Royal Highness would be pleased to order to be paid.

According to the deed, the four hundred pounds "should be paid at or before the ensealing and delivery of these presents," not in installments. The land was described as beginning "at a pile of stones on the Beach at High water mark in a small cove on the North East [sic] side of the North West [sic] Arm, near a battery and boom, and covering 170 acres more or less … excepting and reserving out of the said 170 acres, 25 acres at the North West part of the said tract for the use of the Heirs of the said Jonathan Sterns."

On June 18, 1798, the sale was completed. The deed, duly executed and delivered, was, from then on, in the possession of the imperial military authorities. When the Royal Engineers left in 1906, they took the deed and it was placed among British War Office papers. Only in 1922 was it returned to Canada, to the Royal Canadian Engineers. Lieutenant Harry J. Knight, stationed in Halifax and having custody of military plans and documents, was instructed to register the deed.

On January 23, 1923, the chairman of the Point Pleasant Park Commission, W. A. Black, received a letter from the Halifax law firm, Maclean, Burchell and Ralston. It read:

Dear Sir:

We have been retained by persons representing the heirs of Jonathan Sterns in regard to their ownership of twenty-five acres of land in the vicinity of Point Pleasant Park. If you will refer to the Deed to His majesty the King in 1793 from Jonathan Sterns of Point Pleasant Park, you will note that twenty-five acres at the north-west [sic] corner of the tract were reserved by Mr Sterns for the use of his heirs. This block of land is, therefore, still owned by Mr Sterns' heirs, and neither the Government nor the Park Commission have any interest therein.

We would be pleased if you would take the matter up with your solicitors, with whom we would be glad to confer, and to furnish them with any information required in respect to the title of our clients.

Members of the Commission, who had never heard of the reserved

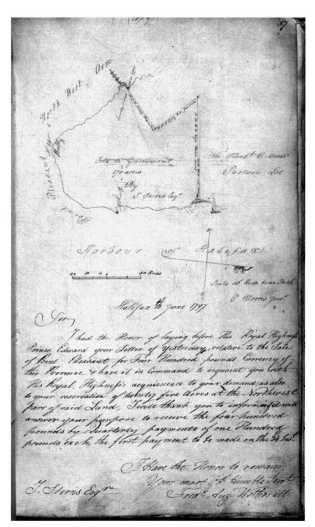

Deed of sale to the Crown of the Sterns land (PANS)

land, expressed surprise and consternation. The chairman, W. A. Black, Commission member Hector McInnes, KC, and the acting city solicitor R. T. MacIlreith, were requested to consult with the city solicitor and report back at a future meeting.

By early February, the startling news appeared on the front page of every local newspaper. The whole story of the original deed was told. The twenty-five acres covered the superintendent's lodge, the gates, the Quarry Pond, Steele's Pond and reached to Francklyn Street.

The claimant was John W. Fraser of New Glasgow. Four quit claim deeds, dated between January and April 1923, were made by heirs of Jonathan Sterns. One deed was signed in January by William Sterns and his wife of Liverpool, Nova Scotia. The next, in February, came from three of Jonathan Sterns' great-grandchildren, who lived in Toronto, Ontario. R. Heber Sterns of Colón, Panama, another great-grandchild, gave up his rights in March. In April, Mary H. Sterns of New York signed her quit claim. According to the document, "In consideration of the sum of one dollar of lawful money of the Dominion of Canada," each heir or "party of the first part hath remised, released and forever quitted claim unto the party of the second part (John Fraser, gentleman, of New

Glasgow) his heirs and assigns."

John Fraser's case, as described by his New Glasgow lawyer before the Halifax firm was engaged, was that there had been no exclusive possession by the Crown, and the park directors had to depend on the Crown's title with only a licence to the property. Once every year, the Crown and Park Commission closed the Park for a day, so there was never a public right to use the Park as common land.

Commission member Mr. McInnes, with a copy of the War Department plans, showed that the twenty-five acres would block all access to the Park from the Tower Road side. The original licence to the Park Commission from the imperial government in 1866 made no mention of any reservation apart from forts. He thought that the Statute of Limitations governing land titles should settle the question. The Park Commission and City of Halifax had sole rights over the property in question for nearly sixty years.

John W. Fraser's claim caused considerable consternation for the Park Commission. Its legal resources were consulted. Fraser's lawyers, both in New Glasgow and Halifax, may not have encouraged him, but certainly took his case. The exact solution was not forthcoming. Park minutes for the period have disappeared. No further references were

found in the Records Office, although a thorough search was made by a legal researcher. Neither law firm has retained documents of the period. Newspapers, as far as could be ascertained, contain no accounts of how the matter was resolved, but it certainly was. The Park did not lose twenty-five valuable acres. What made Mr. Fraser give up remains a mystery.

In a 1913 report written by Frederick W. Cowie to the Minister of Railways and Canals on the proposed new ocean terminals, four alternative schemes were evaluated, with advantages and disadvantages put forward. Scheme D, the one chosen, involved building a breakwater from the shore at Fort Ogilvie into the harbour, a distance of about fifteen hundred feet and "will be built out to and upon a ledge of rock known as Reid Rock, which is at present very close to the surface at low water." It was considered the most suitable site, close to the city with easy and expeditious docking of steamships. Further extensions would be easy with the breakwater simply forming part of the hearting for a complete pier.

Disadvantages included the fact that "Point Pleasant Park will be, to a certain extent, encroached upon.... The area above high water mark of about fourteen acres to be taken from the lands of Point Pleasant Park owned by the Imperial Government

The Park before the ocean terminals'
construction (Kitz)

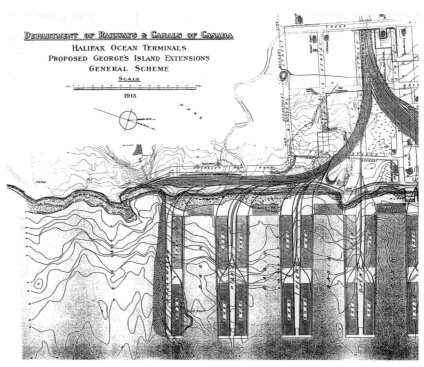

The 1913 plan for ocean terminals (PANS)

and leased to the Park Commissioners." However, the breakwater would compensate for the elimination of the Park's waterfront.

The Park Commission objected, but the land was expropriated, "to the surprise of the Commissioners." Further, the Department of Railways and Canals, without referring to the Commission, placed their railway through park land, filled in a portion of a bathing cove, and cut off public access to the shore for quite a distance. Also, according to the Commission report, the approach to the Park had been made extremely dangerous in consequence of the numerous rail tracks laid across the road. The fence placed close to the Shore Road was decidedly objectionable to the commissioners and the public, and it obstructed access to the breakwater. However, the damage would not be undone, and the Commission requested damages.

In 1890, the Royal Nova Scotia Yacht Squadron clubhouse was built on the Trider estate, just off the foot of South Street, not far from the entrance to Point Pleasant Park. In 1915, two years after the land was expropriated for the new ocean terminals, the clubhouse was demolished. Premier George Murray suggested that a suitable new site would be just outside the proposed breakwater at Black Rock Beach. After the Halifax Explosion of 1917, Brookfield House—a temporary clubhouse—served as the Protestant Orphanage, which had been destroyed, until a new one

could be built. In May 1921, permission to build a clubhouse inside the new breakwater was granted. Objections from the Point Pleasant Park Commission were overruled and construction went ahead.

In autumn 1929, land on Pleasant Street was expropriated for an extension to the ocean terminals, thus closing access to the Park from Pleasant Street. The park commissioners once more claimed for damages. Only after a long controversy was a settlement reached. The government would open, construct and maintain a road from Young Avenue to Pleasant Street near

Right, Royal Nova Scotia Yacht Squadron in Point Pleasant Park (PANS)

Below, view of the R.N.S.Y.S. clubhouse from the water. The shoreline is still wooded. (Jim Bennett)

Steele's Pond, roughly the old Miller Street. A new circular entrance to the Park would be created at Young Avenue. In 1939, the name "Miller Street" disappeared, and the entire stretch became known as Point Pleasant Drive. The Young Gates now stood at either side of the entrance to Young Avenue across the Drive from the Park. The breadth of the Avenue made their function purely ornamental.

In 1959, chairman of the Point Pleasant Park Commission, Gordon Smith, wrote to the port manager of the National Harbours Board, about the Cowie report stipulation that, in return for the loss of land, the Commission would receive certain parking areas for visitors. The property had been gradually filled in and offered splendid views of the harbour, but its state prevented proper use. It was rough graded, with no seawall protection. Mr. Smith suggested installing a seawall, grading its top and laying a pedestrian walkway. The Park Commission would grade, pave and complete the walk if the National Harbours Board would install the seawall. The project was successful and, in the spring of 1961, a stroll on the breakwater became a popular outing. Also in 1959, the swampy area near Point Pleasant Battery had been drained, cleared, then sodded, giving a wide grassy space between the Shore Road and the sea.

Left, the start of the container piers, filling in right up to the seawall. (Jim Clark)

Below, Harbour look-off, entrance to lower car park. The view has been blocked. (Castle)

By 1963, the increasing membership of the Royal Nova Scotia Yacht Squadron made both the premises and the anchorage at the park site inadequate. The decision was made to build a new clubhouse on the Northwest Arm.

The expansion of the Halifax Ocean Terminals in 1968 further encroached on the anchorage. In 1972, when the site had become a financial liability to the club, and no offers were received for its future use, the harbour clubhouse of the Royal Nova Scotia Yacht Squadron was once more demolished.

After extensive negotiation by members of the Yacht Squadron, the lease of their property was transferred to the directors of Point Pleasant Park. Government policy called for a forty-five-year lease at a fee of one hundred dollars per year. As the Park was required to pay that same amount for sewer charges that would no longer be applicable when they took over the land, there would be no extra cost to the annual budget.

By September 1973, the area had been paved and laid out for parking. A stone wall was already built on the park side of the lot. One director suggested planting a row of trees along the high fence to hide it and the shipping containers at the busy pier on the other side. The superintendent reported that plans were already underway. The plentiful parking, close to the ocean, has proved a great asset to the Park.

Earlier in 1973, the Commission had discussed a suitable entrance to the parking area. Chairman Gordon Smith proposed a type of London drawbridge, but professors from the Nova Scotia Technical College (now DalTech) who had been consulted suggested that the design was inappropriate. Two students of the college, Connors and Brooks, had been asked to produce a design. The fountain they proposed was considered too elaborate. Together, superintendent Nickerson and the two students came up with a much simpler design that was approved. The sign on one pillar, "Harbour Look-off," marks the gateway to the car park. At its end can be obtained an unobstructed panorama opening out to the broad Atlantic Ocean.

Past the ocean terminals, the view changes dramatically. (Castle)

3

The Park's Beginnings

Since the founding of the town, the track along the shore to Point Pleasant had provided a favourite walk for the new citizens of Halifax. As early as 1761 a road suitable for carriages existed, but by 1820 parts of it had eroded into the sea, and only a footpath led from the town as far as Steele's Pond. From there the broad track resumed to Black Rock Beach. Paths and roads had developed gradually; many were simply worn tracks and walkways made by frequent use as routes to the forts.

As fear of attack decreased and the military presence lessened, walkers naturally ventured further afield to enjoy the Tower Woods, as the area was generally known, and explore the various batteries.

An article in the *Acadian Recorder* in May 1832 described the anticipated improvements along the shore road to Point Pleasant. "A delightful promenade on the moonlight

Point Pleasant 1840, looking to sea (Mercer Watercolour, PANS)

evenings of next September" could be anticipated. A new wide bridge "built of fine blocks of stone over Fresh Water stream" would connect Pleasant Street (the south end of Barrington Street) with the beach road. The enhancements would be an "elegant" addition to Halifax.

A piece of land owned by the Crown, with no private buildings and within an easy walk of the town, lay at the end of the road. Trees had been cut between the forts and the sea, permitting the strollers fine ocean views from various vantage points. The ocean in all its moods

The road to Point Pleasant
(Watercolour by W. W.
Lyttleton circa 1860, NSM)

The beach road circa 1895 (PANS)

provided plenty of interest. It was rarely empty. There was a wide variety of shipping that plied to and fro across the Atlantic, the only contact with the home country: well-appointed naval vessels, cargo ships—their contents often visible—and immigrant ships with passengers lining the rails, eager to see their new land, small fishing boats and passenger ships that might be bringing home family or

friends. A sunny, breezy day, when the sails were well filled, made a splendid sight. People began to regard the point as if it were their own natural park. In the Halifax *Morning Post* of September 14, 1844, citizens were exhorted to view their improved surroundings with the achievements of industry and crops that had largely succeeded the "stones, brush and rubbish" of earlier times. "For the fresh air, what

better place can be had to quaff the sea breeze than Point Pleasant?"

In 1866, Point Pleasant's status as a park became official. For the next 999 years, the land, subject to certain conditions, would be for public use. Originally, the lease from the Crown to incorporate the directors of a park at Point Pleasant was to be for 99 years, but Chief Justice William Young, former premier of Nova Scotia, future chairman of the Point Pleasant Park Commission, negotiated the extra term.

Chapter 86 of the Acts of Parliament of Nova Scotia reads: "An [Act] to incorporate the Directors of a Park at Point Pleasant, Halifax, Nova Scotia" and was passed May 7, 1866.

Little happened over the next few years. No funding was granted by the City of Halifax as had been anticipated.

In April 1873, a further act was passed, amending that of 1866. One alderman from each ward was to be

CHAPTER 86.

An to incorporate the Directors of a Park at Point Pleasant, Halifax, Nova Scotia.

(Passed the 7th day of May, A. D. 1866.)

1. Incorporation.
2. Directors to obtain license.
3. Company—how organized.
4. Rules.
5. City Council may assess £1000.
6. Military may take exclusive possession.

Preamble.

Whereas, the southern part of the peninsula of Halifax, bounded on the north by lines commencing from the harbor near the stream or water-course about three hundred yards north of Steel's pond, and thence terminating near the old chain battery at the North West Arm, including the lands south of the same to the sea, and known as the war department property, is capable of being laid off and converted into a park, recommended equally by salubrity and beauty of its position, by its proximity to the city, and by the opportunities it would afford to all classes of the community for healthful recreation and exercise ;

And, whereas, there is reason to hope that Her Majesty the Queen, in whom the title is vested, would graciously permit the ground to be occupied and used as a park, subject to the conditions hereinafter contained, and that the necessary funds for its embellishment could be raised by public subscription,—

Be it enacted by the Governor, Council, and Assembly, as follows :

Incorporation.

1. The Honorable William Young, James A. Moren, William Cunard, Andrew M. Uniacke, William J. Stairs, John Tobin, and John Doull, Esquires, and their successors, with the Mayor and Recorder of the City, are hereby constituted a body politic and corporate by the name of the *Directors of the Point Pleasant Park*, with power, in case of the death, incapacity, removal from the Province, or resignation of any one or more of the seven directors first named, to fill up such vacancies from time to time by new appointments, to be entered on their minutes.

Directors to obtain license.

2. The directors shall apply for license to enter upon and occupy the said land as a park, with such reservations for military purposes and defence as the exigencies of the imperial service may require.

Company—how organized.

3. The directors, so soon as they shall obtain license from Her Majesty's Principal Secretary of State for the War Department to enter upon and occupy the said land, shall receive such subscriptions and contributions as may be offered for laying out and embellishing the park, shall appoint a secretary and treasurer, whose office shall be gratuitous, and shall employ suitable persons to superintend and perform the work thereon, agreeably to plans which may from time to time be submitted ; but all such plans, or modifications thereof, shall be subject to the approval of the officer in command of the troops, and the officer commanding the Royal Engineers, at Halifax.

Rules.

4. The directors shall make regulations relative to the maintenance of good order and decorum in the park, the preservation thereof, and the duties of the gate-keeper and other officers, with such penalties as shall be approved of by the Governor in Council ; but no fees or tolls shall be exacted for the use of the park.

City Council may assess £1000.

5. The City Council may assess the sum of one thousand dollars annually, in addition to the present charges authorized by law, and pay the same to the directors, to be applied in payment of the gate-keepers and other expenses connected with the maintenance of the park, and which shall be duly accounted for by the directors.

Military may take exclusive possession.

6. Nothing in this act shall be construed to prevent Her Majesty's Principal Secretary of State for the War Department at any time hereafter from taking exclusive possession of any portion of the said land which may be required for the formation of forts or batteries, or for other military purposes connected with the imperial service.

The 1866 act incorporating the Point Pleasant Park directors. (P. P. P. records)

Sir William Young (PANS)

added to the number of park directors, then reduced to four. City Council would contribute four thousand dollars to the assessment for that year and two thousand dollars for succeeding years to pay for gatekeepers' wages and improvements to the Park. Laying out and maintaining the Park, even with military help, had proved more expensive than first estimated.

Work had already begun on the embellishment of park lands. More than a week before the act became official, the imperial authorities sent a large force of Royal Engineers to remove dead wood, mark out the course of proposed paths and drives and lay out the boundaries. William Young, by then Sir William, had, according to a report in the *Weekly Citizen*, generously advanced four thousand dollars, the sum the city was authorized to assess for the work undertaken

Driving through the Park in winter. (NSM)

A picnic in the Park (PANS)

at the Park so that it should not be delayed.

The *Acadian Recorder* of May 28, 1873, reported that a meeting of the directors of the Tower Woods Park had been held at the mayor's office the previous day. His Lordship, Chief Justice Sir William Young was elected chairman, His Worship Mayor John Sinclair vice-chairman, and Alderman J. S. D. Thompson (future prime minister of Canada) secretary. The vice-chairman and secretary were to confer with the imperial authorities respecting the proprietorship of the park grounds.

A committee, composed of "Messrs Power, Neal, Doull and Stairs," was formed to "wait on the commander of the Royal Engineers to arrange for improvements on the Park."

Strollers now had the added interest of watching busy soldiers, under the command of Major

General H. W. Montague, C.B., creating a new order in the forest, rather than guarding forts or performing military exercises. Eight thousand days of military labour were contributed to make the point into suitable park land. Thereafter, the assessment for park maintenance was set at two thousand dollars per year.

The celebration of the 124th anniversary of the founding of Halifax took place on June 23, 1873, two months after the start of the military labour. It seemed a suitable occasion for the official opening of the Park, and that event was held in the afternoon. Sir William Young, Major General Montague, Mayor James Duggan, the park directors and many citizens made a tour of inspection. The new roads and pathways evoked constant expressions of admiration, and from that summer onward were in regular use.

A public horsecar was available from Halifax as far as Freshwater. From there, a gentle walk along Pleasant Street beside Steele's Pond led to the park entrance. It was also permissible to drive through the Park in a horse-drawn carriage. The favourite swimming place was below Chain Rock, where the chain had blocked the entrance to the Northwest Arm. Pleasant picnic spots, sheltered by the large rounded rocks, added to the amenities.

The last day of 1873, an important agreement was signed regarding the use of Point Pleasant Park (right).

The directors of Tower Woods Park, as the Park was still commonly known, had been in close consultation with Major General Montague throughout the time that his soldiers toiled to create improvements to the woods and trails. Sir William Young could daily be found making tours of inspection and suggestions, taking a great deal of lively interest in the project.

In late February 1875, a special ceremony was held at the Legislative Council Chamber. About sixty ladies and gentlemen were assembled there and were addressed by the mayor and Sir William Young on behalf of the subscribers for a service of plate costing two thousand dollars, to be procured in London as a gift for Major General Montague. The "lady of the mayor" presented him with a handsome silver cup on this occasion. Created by J. Cornelius, local silversmith, at a cost of two hundred dollars, the cup was fifteen inches

AGREEMENT RESPECTING USE OF POINT PLEASANT PARK.

ARTICLES OF AGREEMENT had, made and entered into this Thirty-first day of December, in the year of our Lord One Thousand Eight Hundred and Seventy-three, BY and BETWEEN Her Majesty's Principal Secretary of State for the War Department, of the one part, and the Directors of Point Pleasant Park, duly incorporated by an Act of the Legislature of Nova Scotia of the other part;

WHEREAS, Her Majesty by her Secretary of State of War was graciously pleased in the year One Thousand Eight Hundred and Sixty-six to give Her Royal permission for the use of the Point Pleasant lands at Halifax as a public park on certain conditions expressed and embodied in this Agreement;

AND WHEREAS, The lands consist of the southern part of the peninsula of Halifax, commencing near the harbor of Halifax at the point marked "A" on the annexed plan, thence running west to the point marked "B," thence south to the point marked "C," thence west to the point marked "D," thence south-east to the point marked "E" and thence south-west to the point marked "F" near the Old Chain Battery at the North-West Arm, all which lands are shown on the said plan annexed hereto and are thereon included within a red edging;

NOW THEREFORE, It is by These Presents consented, covenanted and agreed, and license is hereby given that such parts of said lands as are not at present held or may not at any time or times hereafter be required by Her Majesty for all or any Military uses or purposes, defensive or offensive, including the erection of new forts or batteries or other buildings whatsoever, of all which the exclusive possession and control shall remain in and belong to Her Majesty as heretofore, shall and may henceforward be used, occupied and enjoyed by the public and by the said Directors for their use as and for a public Park for the term of Nine Hundred and Ninety-nine years, subject until their determination to existing leases of portions of said lands, and to the conditions following, that is to say :—

1. All plans of proposed alterations, buildings or roads before they shall be commenced or constructed within the said Park are to be submitted for the approval of the General Officer Commanding and the Commanding Royal Engineer for the time being; also a rent of one shilling per annum shall be paid to the War Department for the use of the said Park.

2. The War Department shall have full power to resume possession, without compensation, of any portion of the said lands or buildings whenever it may be required in their judgment for any Military purpose whatsoever.

3. The War Department shall have power to fence in and enclose a sufficient space round the several forts and batteries now or hereafter to be erected on the said land and such portions thereof as now are or hereafter may be required to be occupied as gardens for the troops quartered thereon.

4. The troops in garrison may at any time the General or other Officer Commanding require it march through, manoeuvre or otherwise exercise on the said lands or encamp thereon.

5. The existing main road round the Point together with any new carriage roads that may be formed, shall be maintained and kept in order by the Directors.

6. No establishment for the sale of intoxicating liquors, &c., shall be erected on the said lands in any form without the sanction of the General Officer Commanding, and no building whatever of a permanent character shall be erected without the consent of the said Principal Secretary.

7. None of the trees on the lands shall be cut down for fencing or otherwise and none of the stones quarried without the joint sanction of the General Officer commanding, Commanding Officer of the Royal Engineers and the Directors; but the said Principal Secretary of State shall have power at any time to exercise the right of quarrying stones and cutting down trees or other obstructions in case of necessity and also of cutting sods for the repair of earth works.

8. Any agreement by the Directors for the pasturing or other occupation of the said lands shall be subject to the right of the War Department to resume possession thereof if required for any Military use or purpose.

9. The War Department and the Directors shall severally have the right of closing the Park one day in each year against the use thereof by the public.

10. The said Principal Secretary may re-enter on the said lands on breach of any of the covenants entered into as aforesaid by the Directors, and thereupon this Agreement and all rights and interests of the Directors and of the public thereunder shall immediately determine.

IN WITNESS WHEREOF the said parties to These Presents have hereunto set their hands and seals the day and year first above written.

J. M. C.

EDWARD [L. S.] CARDWELL.
WILLIAM YOUNG, Chief Justice, President.
JOHN A. SINCLAIR, Mayor and Vice-President.
JOHN S. D. THOMPSON, Secretary.

Signed, sealed and delivered by Her Majesty's Principal Secretary of State for the War Department, in the presence of
HENRY ANDREW SOREL,
Colonel.

Signed and delivered under the seal of the within named Corporation, the day and year first above written, in presence of, by the President, Vice-President and Secretary thereof,
JOSEPH SEETON.

Proved by oath of Joseph Seeton at eleven o'clock, A. M., this ninth day of December, A. D. 1875, and registered thereon in the Registry of Deeds at Halifax, Nova Scotia, in Book No. 199, pages 124, 125, 126.
W. H. KEATING,
Registrar.
(Plan is attached to Original on file).

Agreement regarding the use of the Park (P. P. P.)

high. On the lid was a model of a
seven-pounder cannon, with
ammunition complete, sur-
mounted by the intertwined flags
of Britain and Nova Scotia. On the
cup was engraved the Halifax coat
of arms and the inscription,
"Presented to Major-General H. W.
Montague, C.B., by the City of
Halifax, Nova Scotia, in recognition of his valuable services to the
citizens in laying out and beautifying Point Pleasant Park, 1875."
The general accepted the trophy
with suitable remarks and further
suggestions about beautifying
the Park, which would make it the
finest on the continent.

By 1879, Sir William was searching for a suitable tree
nursery in the province. In May he received a letter from
Mr. Israel Longworth, a lawyer in Truro, who had been
asked for advice. He wrote that there was no nursery of
this kind in Truro but that Joseph Henderson of Har-
mony had proved a very successful "procurer and setter"
of trees. He had worked for several well-known people,
and, the description continued, "if not a man of letters,
he was fairly entitled to be called 'a man of trees.' "

Joseph Henderson was able to supply "one hundred
Elms, Ashes and Maples, assorted from eight to twelve
feet high." The cost would be fifty cents each for
maples and twenty cents each for the others. More
could be provided if necessary. If his expenses were
paid to and from Halifax, he would deliver and plant
them himself.

On November seventh of that same year, 1879, the
committee that had been appointed by the park
directors to direct the year's work in the Park, submitted their report. "[T]he shrubs and plants imported last
year from Scotland having been for the most part set

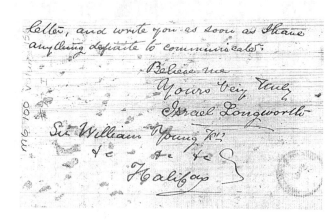

Trees in the Park (early) (PANS)

The park trees, more than one hundred years later (Castle)

out, it was deemed advisable to procure trees from eight to twelve feet in length, and the committee purchased 65 limes, and … 264 ashes, elms and rock maple, 329 in all, which have been planted, and, with a very few exceptions, have taken root and sent forth a luxuriant foliage." Joseph Henderson's offer had been used to advantage. Not only was the committee busily engaged in planting out the Park, but their enthusiasm enabled them to improve the Public Gardens; they directed that the balance of their shrub order—1,430 in all—should be set out there. The report continues:

> The road constructed last year round the extreme
> South point of the Park, and opening up a

magnificent view of the harbor [sic] and the North West [sic] Arm, having been greatly and justly admired, the committee determined to open another road, along the ridge of land east of Fort Cambridge, which has been finished, affording many fine glimpses of the harbor and the opposite shore. The carriage roads, now completed, being perfectly smooth and in thorough order, afford a series of drives greatly frequented by the citizens and resorted to by all strangers. The committee have also improved and strengthened the road at Steele's Pond and removed the keeper, Renner [more correctly, Venner], to the cable house, which passed along with the Park to the Directors, under the Royal grant for 999 years, at a nominal rent, subject to a lease about to expire.

They have recently employed a body of men, under the efficient superintendence of the keeper, to clear out the dead and decayed wood along the principal roads, with injunctions to disturb no living tree or shrub, so as to preserve the native wilderness of the woods, which is one of their principal charms. As this work was observed from day to day by some of the committee, they know that these injunctions were obeyed.

City Council, in view of its financial situation, had reduced the Park's budget from the originally planned $2,000 to $1,000, and the committee had managed to overspend only slightly, $1,058 for the whole year's work. The signatures were those of W. Young, J. W. Ritchie, W. J. Stairs, Thomas Clay and Thos. P. Connolly.

In the spring of 1883, a report from members of the Point Pleasant Park Commission states that fifty trees should be replaced, as they were either broken or dead. Sir William Young once more contacted Israel Longworth to order an additional fifty maple, ash and elm trees. In his reply, Mr. Longworth reported

The results of work on the shoreline road (Kitz)

One of the park roads. All fences were made of lengths of branches. (P. P. P.)

with regret that "the old Forrester [sic]—Joe Henderson—who executed your commission for trees in 1879, is not now in the land of the living." He could, however, recommend another man, from Brookfield.

A further letter, less than a week later, shows that Sir William accepted the substitute. Mr. Longworth informed him that the trees would be dug up a few days later, but that, as elms and ashes

Left, the improved road at Steele's Pond with the cable house beyond circa 1896 (PANS)

Below, the mayor's letter about the park budget in 1883 (PANS)

were scarce, the forester would have to pay for the privilege of lifting them. The cost would be forty-five cents each for ashes and elms, and sixteen cents for maples. The trees would be sent by freight train from Truro, the bill would follow.

The last paragraph of the letter contained the advice that English elms were known to attain their growth sooner and to grow to a larger size than the native species. Fine samples were obtainable from a nursery in Windsor and might do well in the Park.

However, budgeting for improvements to the Park was not an easy task. (See letter to the right.)

Already in 1884, plans were underway to extend South Park Street to create a broad avenue leading to the Park. Properties required for the extension were being appraised by the city. The process proved lengthy, as many of the awards were strongly contested. A letter from Sir William to the

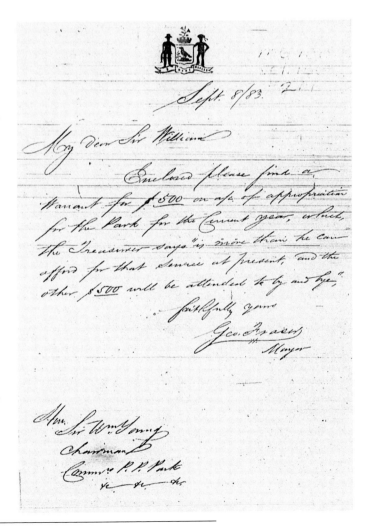

mayor in September 1885 expressed his disappoint-
ment at the road's slow progress. Swamp land had to
be filled and blasting carried out. The city was having
difficulty finding funds to complete the work.

Sir William was becoming worried that he might not
live to see the road's completion. After all, he was
eighty-six years old. He offered an interest-free loan of
fifteen hundred dollars and the work was completed.
Mayor Mackintosh described the new street as the most
magnificent and pleasant approach to the Park, besides
being the handiest.

For some time, Sir William Young had expressed the
desire to contribute fine wrought-iron gates for the
Park, but there had never been a suitable place, only
the accesses to the military roads. The new approach to
the Park, on the height of land between the harbour and
the Arm, giving about three-quarters of a mile of
building sites for quality residences, provided a perfect
official entrance, well suited to ornamental gates.

With the help of the city engineer and a select
committee, Sir William obtained designs from as far
away as Ontario and Scotland. Then, according to his
own statement, he decided that it would be better to
keep the money at home and requested a design from
a local company, Starr Manufacturing of Dartmouth.
When all the designs were examined by the committee,
those chosen were from Edward Elliott for the Starr
Manufacturing Company. As the cost of the gates
proved to be well within the figure Sir William had in
mind, he decided to include massive Nova Scotia
granite pillars. He remarked, "Of course I would not
consent to anything that would not be both handsome
and substantial, and now I think we have secured the
fulfillment of my anticipations."

The city engineer described the plans. The main gate
was to be in two leaves, the granite pillars at each side,
with a single gate to the right and left, each five feet
wide, for foot passengers. The pillars were designed to
be surmounted by lamps if another benefactor could be

Advertisement for Starr Manufacturing of Dartmouth (PANS)

found. (No lamps topped the pillars, so the quest for a
benefactor must have proved unsuccessful.)

The city engineer, asked if the gates were to be kept
open or shut and what would be the real good of them,
answered, "I can't exactly say that they will be of any
practical utility, and I rather fancy an arch or something
of that sort would answer the purpose of an ornamental
entrance better, but it is Sir William's gift and will be a
very substantial one." (The mayor, city engineer and Sir
William were interviewed for a long article in the *Morning
Chronicle* of November 27, 1885, from which the previous quotes are taken.)

On May 26, 1886, there was a gathering of gentlemen at the juncture of Point Pleasant Park and South
Park Street. All the park commissioners were there, as

The chosen park gate design proposal (PANS)

Park gate design that was rejected. (PANS)

well as various city officials. Measurements were made and the ground marked off. Sir William then requested that the commissioners confirm the location and accept the plans for the gates.

The mayor responded on behalf of the Park Commission and citizens, and moved that "the same be accepted with thankfulness towards the venerable donor, who had laid the citizens of Halifax under another debt of gratitude." Nature had endowed Point

Pleasant Park with many scenes of loveliness, both within the grounds and in views of the surrounding scenery, and the mayor hoped that "Sir William would long be spared to enjoy the pleasure to be derived from his connection with the Park to which he had given so much time and attention."

The Hon. Mr. Stairs seconded the motion, adding that it was mainly owing to the exertions of Sir William that the Park had been obtained from the imperial

Above, Young Gates (Kitz)

Left, Park gates circa 1890 (PANS)

Below, the gates lay between Young Avenue and the Park circa 1890 (PANS)

The gates 1996 (Castle)

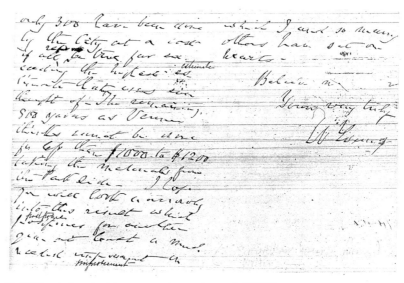
Sir William's handwriting was not easy to read. (PANS)

authorities. It was entirely through his foresight that the lease had been extended from 99 to 999 years.

Sir William, responding in his Scottish accent that he had retained since childhood, gave much of the credit—both for obtaining and putting in order the park grounds—to the generals in command and officers of the garrison. The ceremony ended with three cheers for Sir William.

In the same newspaper interview in which he discussed the gates, Sir William talked about how the Park was run. (He always kept the 1866 and 1873 Acts handy, along with his park accounts, and referred to them often.)

You will notice that three of the original directors remain—Messrs Stairs, Doull and myself—and we look after the management of the Park pretty much between us. Of course the aldermanic commissioners are duly appointed, but they do not trouble us much, being, I suppose, quite confident of our ability. I keep all accounts and have everything under thorough system. Mr. Venner, the keeper, who has proved himself a very good, trustworthy man, gets three hundred dollars a year and his house rent and devotes his whole time to the care of the Park.

He brings me a weekly record every Saturday. I sign warrants on my cashiers for payments and expenses, and things move along smoothly and regularly. I frequently drive through the Park and superintend the keeper's work and see that the balance of the city's little grant of one thousand dollars over the keeper's salary is expended to the best advantage.

He said the synopsis of his accounts would be in the annual civic reports. He mentioned that the sum of five thousand dollars bequeathed by William West, a

Summer house
(Anthony Lugar, Bauld
Collection)

Below, note the
absence of trees around
the summer house circa
1890. (PANS)

POINT PLEASANT.

O'Donnell.

Left, a summer house today (Castle)

Below, a plaque marks the summer houses as gifts from William West. (Castle)

Below left, the park gates ultimately formed the entrance to Young Avenue. (Castle)

wealthy merchant who died in 1881, for beautifying the Park had been of great service.

An account in the *Acadian Recorder* of April 18, 1883, titled "The Park Summer Houses," noted that, on March 30, on board the good ship *Ashantea*, at Glasgow, Scotland, two handsome summer houses had been loaded. A design showing the beauty of their architecture had already been received, and "if they are the equal of the drawing, they will be decidedly handsome." Originally, the design had called for zinc roofs, but the severity of Halifax winters had ruled it out and corrugated iron was substituted. They were manufactured at Walker, McFarlane and Co.'s foundry in Glasgow and were imported for the park commissioners.

According to Sir William, the two pavilions had been erected, and a portion of the bequeathed sum remained to be expended by the trustees. (The balance of the money was used to open a road, known as West Road, at the back of the Park leading from Young Avenue to Steele's Pond.)

The gates were hung on Saturday, August 21, 1886, with some ceremony. The new entrance proved very popular and was much admired. Sir William Young was present when his "Golden Gates" added splendour to the park entrance, and, for a few months, he enjoyed the sight. He died on May 8, 1887. In his will, he left eight thousand dollars to the City of Halifax "to be expended in completing and ornamenting the new road leading from Inglis Street to Point Pleasant Park, and known as Young Avenue." The knowledge, so soon before his death, that the new avenue was to bear his name, had given him great pleasure.

The gates marked the park entrance for more than a half-century, until Point Pleasant Drive was developed during the late 1940s. Afterwards, they formed the entrance to Young Avenue. In 1966, the pillars were moved further apart to accommodate two-lane traffic. Should the gates be closed, which had rarely happened since they were no longer part of the Park, a gap of eleven feet would separate them. In 1999, they were removed for repair.

4
Forts After 1870

Although Pleasant Point officially became a park in 1866, military activities continued for many years. Walkers were encouraged to keep well clear of the forts during times of intensive activity, alterations, repairs or military exercises. Point Pleasant Battery, Forts Ogilvie and Cambridge and the Martello Tower all were occupied by varying numbers of soldiers. Guards were posted at the entrances.

The *Acadian Recorder* of June 15, 1872, reported that once more Forts Ogilvie and Cambridge were undergoing a thorough course of reconstruction. As the twelve-ton guns were being replaced by eighteen-ton cannon, structural alterations had to be made. "Large detachments of Artillerymen and Infantry are encamped in tents at the Point doing this work."

Further developments in coastal defence weapons brought more

ON THE SHORE, POINT PLEASANT, HALIFAX.

Artillerymen practising. (PANS)

rebuilding. In 1888, both forts had concrete mountings installed, allowing two of the new breech-loading guns to be mounted. The underground works in the Cambridge Battery were accessible from a concrete trench behind the guns.

Public use was largely limited to the road along the outer perimeter. A rifle range, used for practice by artillerymen from different units, militia as well as regular army, also saw many a keenly fought competition. The sound of gunfire

Manning the guns at Fort Ogilvie circa 1905. (PANS and Citadel)

Left, the large cannon used for peaceful purposes circa 1890 (PANS)

Above right, practising for war with the same cannon circa 1904 (Citadel)

Bottom, western side of Point Pleasant Park with military wharves on both sides of the Arm circa 1880. Stone from Kings Quarry near Purcell's Cove was ferried across for fort building and repair. (PANS)

frequently discouraged strollers from venturing far into the wooded paths of the interior.

By 1896, when the Martello Tower's usefulness to the military had degenerated, it was decided to install a caretaker. William Smith, a former messenger with the Royal Engineers who had married a girl from Pictou, was happy to settle in Halifax. Most of his ten children had gone out into the world by then. His oldest son's family lived in the guardhouse, away from the main building. One daughter was born there, in very restricted space.

Top, Cambridge Battery circa 1870 looking southwest, showing the stone canteen and earthworks that are part of the gun platform (PANS)

Left, Cambridge Battery magazine circa 1878 (PANS)

Right, Cambridge Battery brick magazine cartridge and shell stores with wooden picket fence 1870s (Public Archives of Canada)

The family entered the tower by climbing the wooden steps to the door in the upper level, which served as living quarters. A dark green curtain gave privacy to the bedroom. Water had to be carried for some distance. In that dark place both heat and light were not easy to supply. Yet grandchildren remember the delicious food and the smell of new baked bread. One granddaughter, Rita, told Sonia Grogono, who interviewed members of the family several years ago and whose notes are used for the personal information, that they were not allowed into the ground floor during World War 1 because of the prisoners there.

In 1922, William Smith died. His son had moved from the guardhouse several years earlier. Mrs. Euphemia Smith stayed on in the tower with one daughter after her husband's death, until she fell down the steep stairs and fractured her hip. She died in hospital in 1925. Since then the tower has had no inhabitants.

During the time that the Smiths lived there, members of the family conducted tours of the fortress with the aid of a candle that cast an eerie light on the dark, rounded walls. Visitors signed their names on the wall of the upper tower, probably to show that they had made the trip up the steep ladder. Before the beginning of the next season the wall was whitewashed, ready for new names.

Top, guardhouse at the Martello Tower. In front stands a corporal of Royal Artillery 1880. The cage at left was used for trapping birds. (PANS)

2nd Scottish Company at the Martello Tower 1883 (Citadel)

Bottom, Martello Tower occupied by a family circa 1910. Note the washing. (PANS, E. Ballenger photo)

Oil painting by Elizabeth Nutt,
1928 (PANS)

Stereo card (the double images
viewed through a stereoscope
would appear as one three-
dimensional image). Note the
inaccurate description. The
tower is British. The errors
continue. (NSM)

95.8.2

6958—Old French Fort, Point Pleasant Park, Halifax, N. S.

This relic of old French days is to be seen in Point Pleasant Park—a delightful resort for the citizens of Halifax, situated on a tongue of land between the harbor and the Northwestern Arm. The Park extends over 160 acres, with paths and drives averaging about fifteen miles.

Until the year 1874, the whole tongue of land belonged to the War Department; but in that year it was generously transferred to the city to be used as a park. Besides the old Martello Tower seen in this picture, four forts and batteries command the coast at different points. Directly opposite, on the west bank of the Arm, stands Fort Redoubt. Near the mouth of the Arm are still to be seen two massive iron rings fastened into the solid rock. From these, in time of war, heavy chains were stretched across to the opposite bank, locking in the harbor and preventing hostile fleets from coming too near the fort to shell it.

The old tower and forts still standing in the peaceful park, have no special legends attached to them, but they are a memorial of the days when enemies hung about the shores in their ships, and blood-thirsty savages sought for the scalps of the men who laid the foundation of this now peaceful Dominion of Canada.

Copyright 1907, by Keystone View Company.

Late in 1905, the Royal Garrison Regiment sailed from Halifax bound for Liverpool, marking the beginning of the imperial troops' withdrawal from Canada. The Royal Engineers followed in 1906 and the Royal Navy in 1907. In January 1906, the Canadian Department of Militia and Defence formally took control of the Fortress of Halifax. After more than 150 years of familiarity with imperial uniforms, people missed seeing them in Point Pleasant Park.

Records show that at the time the British left, Point Pleasant Battery, Cambridge Battery and Fort Ogilvie each contained two of the most recent types of guns, even though by that time there were more modern and better armed forts further out in the harbour.

All of the forts were still partially inhabited, either by regular soldiers, militia or civilian caretakers, some with their families.

When war broke out in 1914, the defence of the city once more gained urgency. Cambridge Battery had already lost one of its guns to Sandwich Battery further out to sea, and neither it nor the Martello Tower was considered of great importance. Throughout the war, the Cambridge Battery's strength consisted of a resident guard from the Composite Battalion, while the Martello Tower continued to be unarmed with only the Smiths in residence.

At the beginning of World War 1, living conditions at Fort Ogilvie were little different from those in the 1870s. (PANS)

In September 1914, soon after World War 1 began, Fort Ogilvie's strength was increased by an NCO and six men of the 75th Regiment, who took over the gun room. A report from a major of the Canadian Garrison Artillery to a captain of the Royal Canadian Engineers in October 1914 stated that there was accommodation in the fort for seventy-one men and three officers.

Most of the buildings in the fort, the barrack rooms, dining rooms, cookhouse, etc., were wooden, but the guardroom, artillery store, latrines and magazines had been more solidly constructed of brick. Facilities were not of the highest standard. The latrines were described in a report as dark and poorly ventilated. One bucket was supplied for officers, one for NCOs,

and two for the much larger number of men. The urinals drained only through a wooden box to the shore. Water for washing was drawn by bucket from a well that was often contaminated and lacking depth. Its water was "sufficient for ablution purposes but makes a poor lather." Shaving with a cutthroat razor in cold, hard water caused many heartfelt complaints. There existed a spring two hundred yards away that was also used by the public, but most of the drinking water had to be brought in by horse and wagon.

By the end of World War 1, sixty-six men were stationed in Fort Ogilvie, which was still considered an important inner defence battery and a backup for the outer forts, such as York Redoubt and Fort McNab. Parts of the barracks served

Fort Ogilvie 1879 (PANS)

as temporary married soldiers' quarters in 1920. The militia still kept a presence there, with accommodation for up to twenty men. Trees were kept trimmed so that visibility was not obscured for gunnery practice. Maintenance and improvements to the various buildings continued to be carried out. The magazine had to be heated year-round to preserve its contents, but in May 1926 a report states that it was nearly empty, and in 1933 troops had been replaced by a caretaker.

Militia authorities had decided to abandon Point Pleasant and Cambridge Batteries by 1936. It took time before their disposal was settled, and the Point Pleasant Park Commission was notified that the areas might then become part of the Park. Inspection of the two batteries in March 1937 revealed "very great destruction of glass and doors, and that, owing to the underground magazines the properties were in a dangerous condition." The Commission declined to take over the batteries unless buildings and fences were removed and danger points razed or filled in. It was certainly beyond the Commission's budget to undertake such work.

Military parties cleaned up to a certain extent. At Point Pleasant Battery the well, cellar and oil storage pits were filled in—precautions necessary for public safety. Cambridge Battery, not considered dangerous, was left as it stood. The Commission still refused to accept responsibility for the forts. Heavy chains, gates and NO TRESSPASSING signs were the military solution.

Two years later, such problems lost significance. The outbreak of World War 2 in September 1939 brought renewed activity in Fort Ogilvie. The 1st (Halifax) Coast Brigade Royal Canadian Artillery CASC moved into the new barrack rooms that were hastily constructed. Members of the Royal Canadian Engineers were well represented as the magazine was restocked and buildings were improved or enlarged. The old complaint of the inadequate supply of good drinking water reappeared in reports. A high fence was erected in December 1939 to prevent trespassing and to make the fort more contained.

Fort Ogilvie had again become part of the defence system for the inner channel, her guns ready to protect against enemy attack from the sea. Through their sights, the gunners could watch the convoys leave the harbour and often see the results of enemy submarine attacks on the merchant ships that limped into port. Newspaper reports made grim reading during the early years of the war. An attack on Halifax did not seem unthinkable. Beside Point Pleasant Battery, two searchlights were mounted and worked in conjunction with the guns at the fort.

By mid-1940, pipes had been installed to provide water to Fort Ogilvie for domestic purposes only—cooking, flush toilets, etc. During 1940 and 1941, the Department of National Defence paved a road through the Park from Tower Road to the fort. Blasting through the rock below to create sewer and water lines was begun in 1943, after complaints from the Park Commission and the city that the above-ground pipes leading to the harbour blocked what the mayor called the "old French road," preventing even firefighting equipment from getting through. In the summer of 1944, authorities believed that the fort lay too close to the city to be effective, so her guns and garrison were transferred to Sandwich Battery to the south, and the rock blasting ceased. A small, mainly caretaking force remained there.

The Martello Tower had been neglected since the Smiths'

departure. Its door stood unlocked. The Park Commission had become worried about its condition and safety. In August 1924, a letter arrived from the Deputy Minister of the Interior in answer to an appeal. The militia, he wrote, had spent vast amounts on improvements to the structure, forsaking its original design. The roof had been removed and a circular gallery installed, "making it more suitable for teas and other social purposes." There was, therefore, no justification for expenditure on it, as there existed many more outstanding sites of national importance.

Various plans for the tower were considered over the years, including a request from a lady to live there and take care of it. An estimate for repairs proved too rich for the Commission's budget and also seemed to make it responsible for the structure, whose care, members argued, should be in other hands. In 1931, a few minor repairs were undertaken by park staff as the Department of Defence refused all responsibility.

The Martello Tower, long boarded up and a worry to the Park Commission, was taken over by the Department of the Interior, the National Parks of Canada section, in 1935. Troubles were not yet over, as the department wished to have a wider area of land around the tower than the Commission approved, an

eighty-foot radius from the centre of the tower. By May 1936, after the transfer was confirmed and agreement reached, work to repair the tower was considered complete, but a wet June caused flooding on the upper floor, and better drainage had to be undertaken.

By 1940, the Department of Mines and Resources, now in charge of the tower, had effected small improvements. The safety of the building improved with the securing of the main door, and a key was lodged with the park superintendent. In 1942, military forces again took over to use the building for storage, and extensive repairs were made.

In June 1946, a year after the war in Europe had ended, Fort Ogilvie, with its twenty-four buildings, was declared surplus to army requirements. Twelve buildings were transferred to the War Assets Corporation. The remainder was to be allocated to the Department of Mines and Resources and maintained by them as a historical site. This may have been the intention at the time, but the transfer did not take place quickly or smoothly. A memo a year later notes that negotiations were only then started for the transfer.

Two official memos in 1946 give permission for army families to occupy certain buildings in the fort as married quarters. A letter from a Royal Engineers colonel to the War

— Photo by Norwood

Inside Point Pleasant Park's Fort Ogilvie

Above, inside Fort Ogilvie (PANS, Courtesy of The Halifax Herald Ltd.)

Decay And Disorder In The Midst Of Beauty

Families lived in Fort Ogilvie (PANS, Courtesy of The Halifax Herald Ltd.)

Assets Corporation, dated December 1946, states that the demolition project at Fort Ogilvie had been satisfactorily completed and the site restored to its original contours.

In June 1947, park superintendent Thomas J. Fripps wrote to the Eastern Command Headquarters of the Royal Canadian Engineers at the behest of the Point Pleasant Park Commission, requesting that Point Pleasant and Cambridge Batteries be removed and the areas levelled off, the barbed wire surrounding Fort Ogilvie also be taken away.

The army responded that it had no further interest in the forts since the war was over. Two military families, however, still lived in the former married quarters in Fort Ogilvie. Army trucks continued to use the roads leading to the forts, their drivers warning pedestrians out of the way, and the heavy vehicles caused some damage to the surfaces. In February 1947, residents were refused permission to have taxis or any type of motorized food delivery to spare further traffic on the fragile roads.

By autumn of that year, one building was vacant. The park superintendent asked permission to have an employee occupy it. He had a large family, and it would be valuable to have him living in the centre of the Park. Permission was given, and the Nickersons moved in.

It seemed only after members of the Commission and the superintendent appeared before City Council and various complaints were reported in the press in February 1948 that the director of Works and Accommodation for Eastern Command began making serious inquiries and plans. The complaints referred to an army dump in one of the forts, unguarded ammunition storage holes, barbed wire, sheet metal and other wreckage, all of which were unsightly and a hazard to park users. Sewage from Fort Ogilvie poured into the sea near Black Rock Cove, where it was proposed to build changing houses. The Park Commission wanted someone to claim responsibility for the forts and the problems that went with them.

In November 1951, after deliberations by the Historic Sites and Monuments Committee, it was decided that three brick and concrete buildings in the Cambridge Battery should be demolished. The demolition would be undertaken as a military exercise by the 5th Field Engineering Squadron, Royal Canadian Engineers Reserve Force. Signalmen, guards and the medical corps were included and, according to the staff writer for the *Mail-Star*, it was a day that "sappers dream of." On November 18, the Park was closed to the public, and, the newspaper report continues, "the

Before and after the attempted demolition of Cambridge Battery (Griswold Collection and Courtesy of The Halifax Herald Ltd.)

shaded paths ... rumbled and shook ... the quiet of the crisp Sunday afternoon shattered by the great blasts and explosions." By the end of the day, the three buildings were rubble. The fort was ready to be restored as a National Historic Site. Further demolition of the same type was discontinued because of public complaints.

More than eight years later, the Park Commission was once more appealing to the federal government to take over the partially demolished Cambridge and Point Pleasant Batteries. An article in the *Mail-Star* of June 9, 1959, describes the disgraceful condition of the forts.

Fort Ogilvie was the most unsightly. Beginning in 1952, it had been briefly used for civil defence training. By 1959, the cannon lay outside the gate, disfigured from an obvious attempt to cut them up for scrap. Nearby were woodpiles, an ash dump, bits of old machinery and much more. A rusty, twisted wire fence surrounded much of the fort. Inside, families still lived in the "converted tarpaper barracks." Signs of fires and vandalism were abundant. The *Mail-Star* article suggested that the Park Commission might well arrange for its own men to clear the garbage from the shore and the dump in Point Pleasant Battery.

In Halifax's Parkland—Not Tobacco Road!

The shore near Point Pleasant Battery (PANS and Courtesy of The Halifax Herald Ltd.)

The article must have made an impact. Ten days later a report remarked that the commissioners and staff were to be commended on the much improved state of Fort Ogilvie. Soon, improvements were also noticeable around the other forts. For instance, a military crane had partly filled the moat at Cambridge Battery. However, the main question of responsibility for the forts' maintenance or removal remained unsettled. The newspaper suggested that if no federal help could be obtained, the city should take over the forts' restoration. Their destruction by explosives or from decay would be shameful.

In 1961, the Martello Tower was declared a National Historic Site. Restoration work began. The interior now holds displays illustrating the history of the tower, which is open to the public during the summer and administered by the Halifax Defence Complex, Parks Canada.

After considerable discussion with the Point Pleasant Park Commission, Fort Ogilvie, Cambridge and Point Pleasant Batteries were taken over by the Canadian Historic Sites division of the Department of Indian Affairs and Northern Development, as it was known at the time. Work began in the mid-1960s, owing to the deteriorating effects of weather and humans. By this time Fort Ogilvie was no longer inhabited. Parts of the forts were mounded over for preservation. Other areas were stabilized. From the Parks Canada Inventory of the Point Pleasant fortifications comes the following information:

Of the North West Arm Battery, little now remains. It is still possible to detect a rough outline of the earthworks of Chain Rock Battery. The small concrete building may have been the anchoring point for the military communication cable.

Top left, erosion by wind and wave, Point Pleasant Battery 1985 (Castle)

Top right, old apple trees survive outside all the forts, and there is still evidence of gardens. (Castle)

Bottom, present-day Point Pleasant Battery (Castle)

Fort Ogilvie retains two gun emplacements, with a shared magazine buried between them, the gate and the 1920 Battery Command Post.

Outside the fort the remains of the submarine mining test room from about 1890 are buried just south of the road to Black Rock Beach. The submarine mining observation station survives intact on top of the hill immediately to the southeast of the fort.

Continued efforts are required if the remnants are to remain. Over the years, the Park Commission had frequent dialogue with Parks Canada under its various names. In 1994/95 a survey of Point Pleasant Battery revealed many weaknesses. Storms and wave erosion, among other factors, are causing damage never brought about by enemy gunfire.

[Text continues on p. 16]

The North West Arm Battery faced the ocean. (Castle)

Below, the North West Arm Battery site from another perspective (Castle)

Fort Ogilvie today
(Castle)

Present-day
Cambridge
Battery (Castle)

Modern drama at Cambridge Battery (Shambhala School)

Dramatic confrontations not once experienced in the height of military days are now a feature of the forts. William Shakespeare's plays provide an exciting spectacle. The Shambhala Middle School gives two performances in Cambridge Battery every June. The latter began with A Midsummer Night's Dream in 1994. Shakespeare by the Sea, now a large professional group, organized by Patrick Christopher and Elizabeth Murphy, also started that summer in a modest manner, giving five performances of Twelfth Night in Cambridge Battery. The endeavour proved such a great success that the next year A Midsummer Night's Dream played for a month. A dramatic, often eerie production of Hamlet was eventually held in the Martello Tower. In the summer of 1996, eighty performances were staged in Cambridge Battery, Fort Ogilvie and the Martello Tower. The latter was also the site of the final act of Macbeth, the action of which took place in different parts of the Park, with the audience following.

Shakespearean performances have proved very popular. Spectators carry their own blankets, lawn chairs and refreshments. Whole families are present, even the occasional dog.

The former park restaurant has become the company's headquarters, the grassy area beside it the site of vigorous rehearsals.

When military engineers designed the fortifications, they envisaged the actions of a theatre of war. Their strongholds, which were never attacked, as stages for Shakespearean battles and dramas would have required a colossal leap of the imagination.

Ophelia in the Martello
Tower (Shakespeare
by the Sea)

Production of *A Midsummer Night's Dream* at Fort Ogilvie (Shakespeare by the Sea)

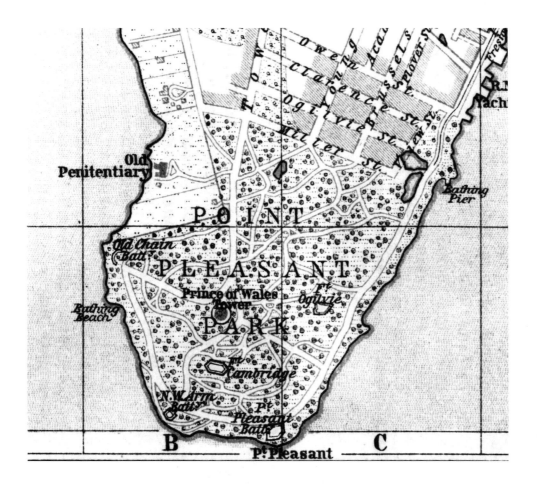

Halifax map circa 1915 showing the Park and forts (Kitz)

5

Purcell's Ferry

Communication and transport among fortifications throughout the city and around the harbour had always been necessary. Various signalling devices served to relay messages. Originally, naval and military vessels were used to convey servicemen and workmen, as well as stone from the quarry near Purcell's Cove, on the other side. A military wharf had been built in the sheltered bay near the entrance to the Arm.

Eventually, in 1853, a regular ferry service for general use, with both row- and sailboats, was set up between Point Pleasant and Purcell's Cove at Island Cove. Initially, the boat was kept at Purcell's Cove and a flag pole at Point Pleasant was used to signal need of its service. However, pranksters found fun in sending false requests for a boat. Joseph Purcell, owner of the boat, tired of wasted trips for non-existent passengers and had a hut built at

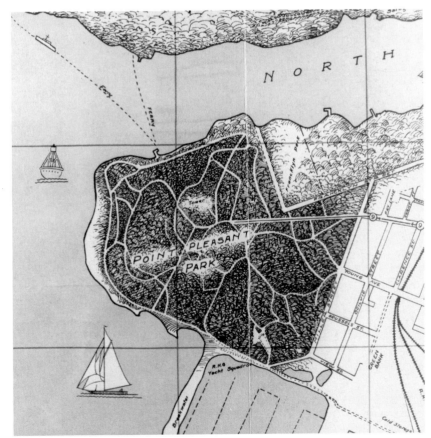

The regular ferry routes (Halifax Regional Library)

Purcell's new ferry house on the Point Pleasant side of the Arm (PANS)

Point Pleasant to serve as a waiting room and contain the flag. In charge was a burly man named Kennedy, who tolerated no nonsense.

When Joseph Purcell died, the service was continued by his son, James, for three years, until he was joined by Robert Carteel (the spelling of his name had been changed from Cartile), who had married James' widowed mother. The commander of the Royal Engineers gave Carteel permission to build a small house on the site of the hut and even supplied materials from old military structures nearby. Carteel and his wife lived in the house and conducted the ferry from the Point Pleasant side, while James and Samuel Purcell ran the operation from Purcell's Cove.

The service did not always meet with approval. In August 1878, one

The Purcells' ferry house circa 1892 (John Barrington watercolour, PANS)

dissatisfied customer wrote to the *Morning Chronicle*:

> It is very generally known among persons who frequently have to cross by ferry, rather late, to York Redoubt, or the neighboring villages on that side of the North-West Arm, that they have to return disappointed, owing to the present worthy proprietor of the ferry being unable to take them across, he offering the excuse that the water is too rough. Consequently, persons have to return to town, a mile distant, no matter how necessary it is for them to cross at once. I propose that the military men now stationed at the Point for the purpose of preventing their brethren in arms from proving false to their colors by making their exit from that place, should act as ferrymen, the fare to be the same as at present, and the boats to be provided out of the needless expense already entailed in paying the ferryman on that side of the Arm, thereby promoting convenience by placing work in the hands of men who are not afraid of rough water. Trusting this may meet the eye of someone interested in the matter who can further its adoption,
>
> I remain,
> Pro Bono Publico.

Purcell brothers' report on one year's ferry traffic (Carol Anne Janc)

Evidently the letter did not meet an appropriate "eye."

In 1880, Major W. A. Purcell, well known as a taxidermist, took over the Point Pleasant service and his brother, Charles, ran the Island Cove side. The boats carried Her Majesty's mail year-round, but summer was the busy season, with Spectacle Island in Purcell's Cove a very popular destination for picnics and swimming expeditions.

In 1890, the whole service came under the control of Robert J. Purcell, who ran it entirely from Point Pleasant. By this time, the ferry house was dilapidated, and the site itself was not the most suitable as it was exposed to the weather. The ferry had become more of a local convenience since the military now had their own vessels for service among the forts. The Purcells had regular passengers, who travelled by ferry to work or to shop and also those who used it for pleasure trips.

The ferry service had come under the supervision of the Point Pleasant Park Commission, which paid a small subsidy to supplement the fares. In the early days, the imperial government had done the same to pay for the transportation of troops. In 1909, the same year that motorboats came into use, the Commission decided to build a new cottage and wharf on the more sheltered bay further into the Arm, where the military wharf had stood. The structures were completed in 1911, and a telephone was installed for public safety. In one cottage or another, Robert James Purcell's twenty-one children were raised.

William R. Purcell, at the age of sixteen, took over the ferry service from his father in 1916, and personally ran it, along with a tuna operation in the summer. (Commercial fishing helped to supply the ferryman with a livelihood. Lobster

The military wharf (Anthony Lugar, Bauld Collection)

and tuna provided the more lucrative harvests.) He also eventually ran a service to McNab's Island for picnics and camping trips. The fare for a one-way crossing was fifteen cents. On a fine Saturday in the summer, about thirty people would use the ferry, and the owner stated that, weather permitting, he never refused a fare.

A 1934 Park Commission report noted that the lease of the ferry house to the licensed ferryman was one dollar per year. The tenant was to make internal repairs and keep the grounds in order. In the early 1950s, the rent of the cottage remained one dollar per year.

Commission records note that the ferryman was very useful in fire

The ferry house had become dilapidated. (PANS)

The 1911 new cottage with boat tied up at the new wharf (Carol Anne Janc)

prevention. He also still held the franchise with the provincial government for carrying mail across to Purcell's Cove. William Purcell (known to park regulars as Bill), his wife Theresa, and three children, Cora, Catherine and Aubrey, lived in the cottage. Later, both girls married and left. Aubrey helped to run the ferry service and small canteen.

Mrs. Purcell, with her ice cream and pop sales, rarely had an uninterrupted meal during the summer. The cottage and surroundings were often busy. Racers from the Armdale Yacht Club would arrange to have large supplies of sandwiches at the Purcells'. Bill was frequently called upon to render first aid for scrapes and cuts or to remove fishing flies from fingers or other sensitive areas. His ghost tales, many based on his own experiences, thrilled more than one generation of local

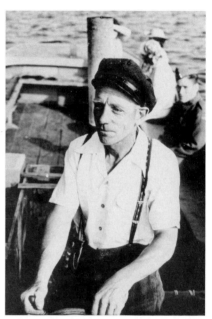

From left to right: Bill and Theresa Purcell's children Cora, Cathy and Aubrey (Eric Melvin)

children and some adults. A newspaper report described an incident that took place in 1960. Bill Purcell "makes a habit of extracting would be victims from the waters of the North-West [sic] Arm…. [He] saved a boater by grabbing him by the hair and pulling him to safety."

Carol Anne, their granddaughter, spent days with her grandparents, helping to serve ice cream. She even learned to steer the ferry and take compass readings on the numerous crossings she made with her grandfather. At Christmas and Easter, her parents received special permission from the Park Commission to drive their cars all the way to the Purcell cottage when they arrived laden with gifts.

In November 1963, the question of continuing or terminating the Purcell lease was discussed by the Point Pleasant Park Commission and was also brought before City Council. The mayor suggested that the ferry had outlived its usefulness. Robert Kanigsberg, member of the Park Commission, claimed no service was being provided to the city; the ferry's canteen competed with the official canteen concession at the beach entrance; the Purcell family drove the only private cars in the Park; and taxpayers were paying for the upkeep of the building. (Mr.

Capt. Bill Purcell (Carol Anne Janc) and Theresa Purcell, his wife (Eric Melvin)

Left, boarding the ferry (Carol Anne Janc)

The ferry was popular for outings. (Carol Anne Janc)

Purcell received a provincial subsidy of four hundred dollars per year.) Mr. Kanigsberg finished, "I don't think the city owes any loyalty to the children, grandchildren or great-grandchildren of someone who rendered a service a number of years ago." The motion to end the lease the following March was passed unanimously.

Public outrage resulted. Letters appeared in every newspaper. Telephone calls to City Hall and the Park Commission expressed extreme indignation. Headlines described eviction. One article referred to the Commission's "unexcelled record of constructive policies and real achievements." Only unawareness of the true

situation could possibly explain such a decision.

For the past few years, the city had been spending ten thousand dollars each summer for a Northwest Arm safety patrol. Boating was increasing greatly in popularity, and the patrol could not be at both ends of the Arm at once. Since the patrol began, Bill Purcell was

Dominion of Canada

Province of .... N.S.

County of .... Halifax

In the matter of rescue from .... Drowning ....

of .... Adults ....

I, ... Wm R Purcell .... of the .... Ferry .... of .... Halifax .... County

of .... Halifax .... Province of .... N.S. .... Dominion of Canada, do

solemnly declare that .... I made these rescues from Ferry boat

Those are the names of the rescues. and witnesses.

		Witnesses
1919 —	3 men upset by Bell Buoy. —	Mrs Chapman – Earl Purcell
1919 —	Mr Southgates. 4 Students. Red Buoy —	Wm Murray.
1924 —	Mrs (Major) Edwards. Purcells Cove –	Stanley Purcell.
1924 —	4 Soldiers in row Boat. Purcells Cove. —	Stanley Purcell, Soldiers
1926 —	2. Young Men in Dingy Red Buoy. —	Wm Murray.
1928 —	3 Students from Pine Hill. N.W.A —	Harold Perks
1944 –1	Sailor in canoe. 2 boys and 2 girls. Quarry Ries.	Wm Gill
1944 —	Mr Roy Ward in canoe middle of N.W.A — Roy Lynch – W Landry. L. White
1944 —	2 Sailors in yacht by red Buoy — Wt Purcell – E. Chapman.
1944 —	2 Sailors in Dingy Red Buoy mens from Kings College — C Lowas
1944 —	2 Naval Ratings in canoe. york pier — Ed. Chapman. R.N.C.V.R.
1944 —	4. in Blue snipe. 2 Boys–2 girls. N.W.A—John Currul – Cambridge Mass

And I make this solemn declaration conscientiously believing it to be true, and knowing
it is of the same force and effect as if made under oath and by virtue of the Canada Evidence Act 1893

Declared before me at the

.... of ....

County of ....

This .... day of .... 194 ....

Lives saved by Bill Purcell (Carol Anne Janc)

credited with saving more than twenty lives because of his own initiative. The ferries and workers had contributed significantly to the safety of sailors and swimmers during the years of operation, when they were the only full-time boat operators in the area. Still, during most of the year, the Purcells were the sole providers of a life-saving service. William Purcell kept a little red book in which were the names of the 135 people whom he had pulled from the water during his half-century at the Park.

His most recent boat was a nine-passenger Cape Islander that carried an average of five thousand

Aubrey Purcell at the wheel of *Tana* (Carol Anne Janc)

passengers a year. The canteen was a favourite place of many local youngsters, who had questions about fishing and boats, and listened to stories about the Northwest Arm and rescues as they drank their pop or licked their ice cream cones. Boaters asked for advice when they stopped for gas; the Purcells' many years of experience proved invaluable.

Mr. Kanigsberg's other arguments for shutting down the ferry service were also easily answered. As far as the canteens were concerned, their situations meant that they had entirely different customers. Let official status be given to the protective work that the Purcells had always carried out unofficially and voluntarily. A car was a necessity to carry rescued persons to hospital. An appointment as life-saver with free rent of an old house would

seem little enough compensation. What a sorry end to years of wonderful service this eviction would make.

Within days, the Point Pleasant Park Commission appointed a two-man committee to negotiate a new lease with William Purcell. In April 1964, after a meeting attended by all commissioners, the new terms were announced, although agreement was not unanimous. Commercial operations are against park regulations. William Purcell would be allowed to maintain fuel pumps on site and to continue his tuna fishery, as it was considered a tourist attraction. The small canteen outlet, which had existed for more than sixty years, would also remain as a public service. However, he would no longer be allowed to land lobster or to transport them through the Park for commercial purposes, nor could he store any

boats on the premises, except those used in his own business. The lease would terminate upon Mr. Purcell's wish or upon his death. The rent would continue at one dollar per year, but Mr. Purcell would pay residential and business taxes. Previously no assessment had been made, but it was set at $298.

For the next few years, the Purcell family continued with their work. Aubrey took over more of the duties as his father's health deteriorated. He also fished, mainly tuna and lobster. He was a great yachtsman as well as an expert fisherman and had served in the RCAF marine division during World War 2. His expertise and knowledge kept him in demand to escort parties of anglers on fishing expeditions. Under contract to the provincial government, he had conducted a survey of tuna in the

Right, the Hen and Chickens rocks where seals often bask (Castle)

Below, the Purcell home in 1971, just before they left (Carol Anne Janc)

visibility, forcing the divers to give up shortly after midday.

The previous evening the National Harbours Board policeman from the Coast Guard had reported that an outgoing boat had spotted a man floating near the breakwater by the container pier. It was believed he was wearing a life jacket.

On Monday morning, Eric Melvin, Aubrey's brother-in-law, spotted Captain Aubrey William Purcell's body among the Hen and Chickens shoals. It was brought to the surface by naval divers.

In September 1971, a few months after the death of their son, the Purcells vacated the premises. The Commission decided that the property should be demolished and the land made into a picnic area. In October, during an official ceremony, a framed photograph of the house was presented to the family, a small memento to mark 118 years of Purcell service to the community and a colourful fragment of the Park's history.

St. Margaret's Bay area and another area off Prince Edward Island.

In May 1971, disaster struck. On the evening of Saturday the eighth, Aubrey Purcell's empty fishing boat was found drifting off the shore of Point Pleasant Park. The motor was in neutral but still running. A search started, conducted by the Department of Transport pilot boat, and a navy launch soon joined. The search, called off at nightfall, resumed the next morning, when navy divers were also called in. Their investigation centred on the area of the Hen and Chickens rocks, where Aubrey had been attending lobster traps. Water conditions hampered

The plaque in memory of the Purcell family, dedicated October 1971 (Carol Anne Janc)

Above, Bill Purcell and family at the dedication of the Purcell memorial (Carol Anne Janc).. Left to right, Stephen Burke (grandson), Theresa and Bill Purcell, Sharon Burke (grand-daughter), Craig and Carmen Janc (great-grandchildren), Cora Melvin (daughter), Carol Anne Janc (granddaughter), Cathy Burke (daughter) and Sean Burke (grandson).

Memorial to Cathy, Bill's daughter (Castle)

THIS PLAQUE IS DEDICATED TO
WILLIAM PURCELL
BY THE ARMDALE YACHT CLUB
IN GRATEFUL APPRECIATION FOR SAVING
THE LIVES OF FIFTY PERSONS FROM
DROWNING IN THE WATERS OF THE
HALIFAX HARBOR AND THE NORTH WEST ARM

The plaque dedicated to Bill Purcell was presented to the Maritime Museum of the Atlantic by son-in-law Darrell Burke in 1999. (Castle)

Below, the cottage and ferry house are now gone. (Castle)

6

The Ponds

Two ponds feature in Point Pleasant Park history. The Quarry Pond, situated to the rear of the lodge and workshops, was so named as it was the result of quarrying stone for the construction of early forts. The pond's depth varies according to the season and amount of precipitation. In a dry summer, little remains but a large puddle of shallow, muddy water with sparse stunted water lilies still visible. Often the Quarry Pond has been revived by the addition of water supplied by hoses from the nearby park buildings or even by the fire department.

In winter it freezes quickly, becoming a popular site for young skaters and ice hockey enthusiasts. In spring one can usually find tadpoles and a few frogs, sometimes because nature lovers have made sure that the pond was stocked. Water lilies come into bloom in early summer. A few black

The Quarry Pond circa 1875. In the military cottage lived an old soldier named Garrety, of the Royal Engineers. (PANS)

duck frequent the pond as long as there is enough water for them.

The Quarry Pond is also associated with tragedy. Just south of the Dominion Penitentiary that stood on the shore of the Northwest Arm was the farm of Robert Maitland.

His son drowned in the pond in the mid-1860s, just before the land was designated a park.

In June 1889, the depth of water in the pond may have been greater than usual. A newspaper reported that it was the wettest spring on

The Quarry Pond circa 1995. The park lodge is to the rear. The bridge was designed and built by park staff. (Castle)

Below, the Quarry Pond in summer (Castle)

record. On June 6, the *Morning Herald* printed a detailed account of a suicide in the Quarry Pond. The wife of the principal of Victoria Art School had left her home on Victoria Road after kissing her children and giving the eldest, an eight-year-old, her engagement ring. The search for her, which ended at the Quarry Pond, revealed her umbrella and hat floating on the surface. A pole was used to try to reach another object without success. The husband, quoted as saying, "I am a good swimmer," plunged into the water. The object was actually a rock showing above the surface. Eventually, her body was recovered from the pond.

An inquest attributed the suicide to temporary insanity. A rider added to the verdict strongly recommended draining and filling Quarry Pond as it had been the scene of too many tragedies. At that time, no lodge or outbuildings stood near the pond. Trees surrounded it, making it a much more secluded spot.

In November of the same year, a short paragraph appeared in the *Acadian Recorder*, noting that, at last, the Quarry Pond was being drained and filled. Men were engaged in the work all day, using old boughs and tree stumps to fill the pond. These materials were later removed and the pond continues to exist.

More than four decades later, the Quarry Pond was once more the site of pleasant recreation. In 1934, blasting was carried out to remove stone and enlarge the pond "to make it better for kiddies' boat sailing." In April 1959, it was noted that there had been sixty-five days of skating.

Steele's Pond lay just outside the Park, at the lower entrance, south of Greenbank (the settlement at the south end of Pleasant Street). There are two theories about this pond's name. The more prosaic is that it was named after John Steele, who came to the area in a group with Edward Cornwallis in 1749. By 1752, he was living in the south suburbs of the new settlement, not far from the pond. Later he moved to Annapolis and became MLA for his area. The more dramatic and tragic source of the name was an early settler named Steele, who drowned there and whose body was never recovered. Either trapped in the pond's murky depths or mysteriously washed out to sea, the body disappeared.

It was, according to season, a popular place for skating, boating and other recreation. Tired horses were often led there to drink the fresh water and cool off.

An article in the *Acadian Recorder* of January 9, 1878, gives this description:

Whoever has gone to or come from Point Pleasant by the lower road must have been struck by the dangerous nature of the passage at Steele's Pond. On the one side of a somewhat narrow road, is the pond, with a depth of from five to seven feet of water near the edge, and on the other the shelving beach leading to the sea. A sudden bolt on the part of a spirited horse, and before it could be controlled the occupants of a vehicle might be in the water on one side or the other. Whether the sad accident to be recorded this morning happened from the unprotected condition of the roadway will probably never be known, as death seals the lips of all who could have told.

The day before, early in the morning, John Thomas, a gas company employee, found a horse and sleigh on Inglis Street. The horse had lost both bridle and bit, the reins were broken, and a fur robe that obviously had been soaked lay frozen stiff in the sleigh. Calmly, Mr. Thomas led the horse to his company's works, then went back to his job of putting out the gas lights along Inglis Street. Afterwards, he took his find to the police station.

The owner of livery stables had spent the night looking for the sleigh and driver, a man he regarded

Steele's Pond and Pleasant
Street as it continued into the
Park (Kitz)

Below, Greenbank and
Steele's Pond circa 1896.
Situated close to the road,
Steele's Pond could pose
problems. (PANS)

Steels Pond & Entrance to Park. Halifax, N.S.

THE GREEN BANK ENTRANCE TO POINT PLEASANT PARK, HALIFAX, N. S.

The rowing team at Steele's Pond circa 1874 included (from left to right) Wm. Ross, R. Foley, John Mann and Mike Inglis. (PANS)

Skating at Steele's Pond (PANS)

highly and had employed for several months. Later that day a rug and whip were found at Steele's Pond. Quickly a search of the pond was started, made difficult by its frozen state. Then came more dreadful news. Two girls were missing. By nightfall their bodies had been recovered fairly close to shore, but there was no sign of the driver. There were two broken places in the ice, as though the horse had gone through but had managed to pull out again. The driver's badge and hat lay on the ice.

The driver, Wilson, had been on the stand soon after eight-thirty in the evening and was hired by the two girls. No one was sure of their movements after that. Possibly he had driven on to the ice as the roadway along Steele's Pond was uneven and boulder-strewn after recent storms. It was also common practice to drive over the pond when it was firmly frozen and bearing.

The search for Wilson's body continued, hindered by the necessity to cut holes in the ice to look into the depths. On the afternoon of the second day, after rumours that the young man had been seen alive and well in Herring Cove, his body was found at the same time as the funeral procession for the two girls.

Park Commission minutes of December 1893 note: "The condition of the piece of water known as Steele's Pond has long been a matter of anxiety, from its dangerous depth in some parts, and the precipitous character of its bank along the principal public drive." As a result, the following winter, the Commission took advantage of the very severe frost that had formed thick ice on the pond. Three thousand loads of stone were carted onto the ice over the deepest parts, which had been marked off. When the ice thawed, the stones reduced the depth by four or five feet. It cost about six hundred dollars, and a

Wilfred Creighton testing a fire pump at Steele's Pond 1934. Greenbank is built up and the pond much diminished compared to the 1896 photo. (Dr. W. G. Creighton)

further four hundred dollars were to be spent on a similar project when the water froze early in the next year. A dangerous part of the pond was fenced using waste wood chopped in the process of thinning.

In 1916, the Halifax Ocean Terminals engineer and a representative from their construction company approached the Park Commission about having Steele's Pond filled in. The Commission refused but strongly supported the idea of raising the level of the road.

A drawn-out controversy was settled in 1924 after the government expropriated Pleasant Street to accommodate the railway terminal expansion. Access to the Park from Pleasant Street was closed off. The Commission agreed to withdraw their claim to the land in question in return for the government's agreement to open, construct and maintain a road from Young Avenue to Pleasant Street near Steele's Pond. Since the plan affected Greenbank it caused some disagreement but was eventually carried out.

In 1945, the amount of rubbish around Steele's Pond dismayed the Commissioners. The mayor agreed to write to the port manager to suggest draining the pond. Two years later, a letter from the port manager asked if the Commission wanted Steele's Pond drained, filled in, and the area made suitable for traffic. He believed that considerable opposition would result. Instead, the Commission pointed out that the pond was already

A modern view: Steele's Pond no longer exists. (Castle)

practically gone and suggested that the National Harbours Board complete the job. A culvert should be constructed for drainage. In 1951, the work commenced, and Steele's Pond was no more.

7
The Beaches

Chain Rock Beach (Collection of Brian Cuthbertson)

During the nineteenth and early twentieth centuries, the favourite bathing place was near Chain Rock, where a public bathhouse stood. A 1915 guidebook to "Pleasant Drives Around Halifax" describes Chain Rock Beach as "delightfully situated and well equipped." Bathing towels and clothes were available at a nominal charge.

A sewer outlet spilling into the Arm, after housing development in the surrounding area, made Chain Rock Beach less inviting.

Black Rock Beach, lying in a bay originally sheltered from the worst of gales and heavy seas by the black rocks, is now also protected by a long breakwater at the end of the container pier. In the early days of the Halifax settlement, a gibbet stood for a time at the end of the beach. As a warning to prospective evildoers, a pirate's decaying body was once left there for several months.

Right, picnic at Chain Rock Beach circa 1900 [Mrs. Janet Piers, Kathleen (Holmes) MacNeill album]

Below right, sewer outfall near Chain Rock Beach, 1998 photo (Castle)

Chain Rock Beach from the water (Castle)

Modern-day Chain Rock Beach. Swimming was prohibited 1990. The iron ring is out of sight on the left. (Castle)

The horse heads for Black Rock Beach, passing the people at Steele's Pond. (PANS)

The gravel beach at Black Rock became the popular bathing resort, and not only for humans. At dawn and sunset, grooms and truckers would ride along Pleasant Street to water their horses at the nearby stream and might then urge the tired animals into the cool sea to refresh them.

Fine summer days drew many picnic parties to the shore. At the end of 1938, the Park Commission received a letter strongly recommending that the popular beach area should be sanded. The idea was well received and the means would be investigated. However, a summer's delay brought the outbreak of World War 2, and, once

The first changing houses, 1940s. In the background, the Royal Nova Scotia Yacht Squadron clubhouse. (Collection of Edgar (Sonny) Boutilier and Courtesy of The Halifax Herald Ltd.)

A busy day at the beach 1955 (E. G. L. Wetmore photo, NSM)

more, the Park changed dramatically. Military uniforms and vehicles abounded in the roads leading to Fort Ogilvie, which had a full complement of militia and engineers. Citizens were actively discouraged from using the beach by 1944, when sewage from Fort Ogilvie had polluted the water.

In the spring of 1948, the fort had only a few inhabitants, and sewage was no longer considered a major problem at Black Rock Beach. It was decided that changing houses and a boardwalk would be built by the park staff. The project was deferred, pending a report on the condition of the water. That proving satisfactory, it was carried out.

The question of sand came up for discussion again in September 1949. One Park Commission member, Mr. Briggs, agreed to inquire of shipowners whether sand that had been used for ballast could be secured and placed on the beach. At no cost, Mr. Briggs obtained 150 loads of the sand, which was spread in time for the 1950 swimming season, adding a foreign element to the native gravel.

The sandy beach proved a great success, so the Commission decided to enlarge it. The following summer, a large quantity of sand was donated by Hubley's Sand and Gravel Company. The Standard Paving Company offered to trans-

port and unload it onto the beach free of charge. Building sand castles soon became part of the charm of a day out at Black Rock Beach.

During the summer of 1952, the Park Commission hired a lifeguard. The particularly fine weather that year drew crowds to the beach. Families carrying beach gear, eager to play in the sand and sea, filled the bus that ran from Tower Road to the park entrance at Black Rock. On Sundays and holidays a shuttle service ran between the two points. The Commission then considered a swimming pool, and the long-delayed changing houses were to become a reality. The swimming pool idea was turned down, but

Improvements at Black Rock Beach included the stone wall going off at an angle to the right and a new boardwalk passing in front of changing cabins and on to the protective rocks. (Castle)

Below, the sandy beach was popular in the summer. The new walls, built by park staff, formed its boundary. (Charles P. Burchell, PANS)

more sand was added for the following summer at a cost of three hundred seventy-five dollars for five hundred gallons. A diving board, constructed by the park staff, gave access to deeper water and was well used.

In 1953, a YWCA camp held swimming classes at Black Rock Beach for one hour a day. These classes continued for several years. On July 5, 1953, it was estimated that six thousand people were in the Park, most of them at the beach. In August, rather late in the season, ten permanent changing houses were at last under construction. The lifeguard was paid thirty-five dollars per week. Eventually the guard was provided free by the City Recreation Department. In the summer of 1955, washrooms were built close by, completing the amenities.

In the early 1960s, many plans were considered for upgrading and extending the beach area. Experts were consulted and indicated it might be possible to extend and enlarge facilities to accommodate thousands of swimmers and to provide extensive diving facilities. Work continued annually, and by July 1962, the beach was larger by a third. Rocks and a new stone wall enclosed much of the sandy area. The walkway along the breakwater had been completed a year earlier, the boardwalk in the late forties.

A new boardwalk on the elevated level in front of the changing cabins led out to the rocks that provided shelter from the Atlantic storms. By 1964, the beach had become

Top, Black Rock Beach rock concert 1965 (Castle)

The new changing houses 1972 (Castle)

twice its original size. The nearby canteen was serving an average of two hundred lunches a day the following summer.

At the Halifax Natal Day picnic in July 1965, an afternoon rock and roll concert and dance was held at the beach from two o'clock till five. For more than twenty years, the concert continued as an annual event until 1990, when it was less successful—the surroundings were partially damaged.

The advent of more plentiful swimming pools, the usually cold temperature of the beach water and its increasing pollution along with readily accessible transport for expeditions further afield have discouraged modern swimmers, except for the very hardy ones who take the plunge at the annual Polar Bear Swim on New Year's Day, a tradition since 1975.

The Polar Bear Swim at
Black Rock Beach 1996
(Castle)

Crowds of spectators attend
the Polar Bear Swim (Castle)

The summer of 1993 saw the last
lifeguard on duty. No further funds
would be available from the Department of Recreation. A report noted
that the lifeguard's duties had been
minimal. Most users of the beach
were sunbathers, whose lives were
in no danger from the ocean.

By 1995, the row of changing
cabins had not been used for its
original purpose for some time, so
the Park Commission decided to
have it removed. The improvement
in the view has evoked exclamations
of pleasure, especially from early
morning walkers, whose first sight-
ing of dawn spreading its colour
over the ocean is no longer im-
peded by the unattractive structure.

By 1993, the beach was rarely used for swimming. (Castle)

The removal of the cabins in 1995 improved the view. (Castle)

8
The Heather

The origin of the spreading heather patches, giving their show of brilliant purple in late summer, has caused controversy over the years. In August 1878, the correspondence column of the *Morning Chronicle* featured several letters on the subject.

One, signed by "Sandy and Jock," quoted from transactions of the Institute of Natural Science of April 10, 1876. At that time Professor Lawson stated, "It subsequently became known that there were several patches of heather at a particular spot in Point Pleasant Park, and although much of it has already been taken away by inconsiderate persons, yet it still exists…. One suggestion [regarding its origin] was that the Highland soldiers encamped there some thirty or forty years ago used heather brooms for sweeping out their camps and the seeds had dropped from the brooms and given rise to the heather patches." After examining the site with a colleague, however, he came to the conclusion that it had been deliberately planted and cultivated. He was certain that it was not an indigenous variety.

Sandy and Jock were apparently annoyed by a previous correspondent who had asserted that there had been huge tracts of heather in North America long before the existence of Scotland. These plants, in his opinion, were the last, not the first, in the province. Changes must have taken place, possibly in climatic

(Mary Primrose)

(Mary Primrose)

The heather casts a purple haze. (Gary Castle)

Highland soldiers used heather brooms. (The Trustees of the National Museums of Scotland, 1999)

conditions, denuding this continent of heather, but permitting it to continue to flourish in Scotland.

Another participant in the argument claimed to have seen heather growing six feet high in Ireland. Scotland, he wrote, could not claim the sole right to the heather. It might equally well be English, Irish, Welsh or Nova Scotian.

Sandy and Jock ended their letter, "Reasons have been given why the heather in question may be regarded as 'Scotch heather.' " On the question of it being Scandinavian or Irish they added, "We can conceive of a son of Erin bringing over a shamrock and planting it, not, certainly, a sprig of heather or a thistle. We would leave that for the Scots."

On August 29, 1889, the obituary of John H. Johnson appeared in the *Halifax Herald*. One sentence stands out: "It was he who planted the patch of 'heather' on Point Pleasant

The Black Watch (Postcard by Harry Payne)

Park—a rarity which is the surprise and joy of Scotchmen."

An article in the *Dalhousie Review* of 1928/29 by Edward Prince discusses different theories on the origin of heather in the Park. The first was that Sir William Alexander introduced it in 1621 to create a New Scotland, as there already existed a New France and New England. (Sir William Alexander, later First Earl of Stirling, received a land grant of the whole of Nova Scotia from James I of Great

Britain. He created, for a fee, the baronets of Nova Scotia. Each baronet was required to send to the colony six men, fully armed and equipped for two years. Scottish colonists were sent to Port Royal in 1620 to settle the new land, but the attempt was abandoned in 1631, and France regained possession in 1632. It was never confirmed that heather had accompanied the group, or even that anyone had ever reached the site of the future Halifax.)

According to Mr. Prince, other authors have credited the Black Watch regiment. In the spring of 1757, the famous "Forty-Twas" camped at Point Pleasant. Some of the soldiers planted the heather seed to perpetuate the badge of many of their clansmen.

Folklorist Helen Creighton found a reference that sounded quite definite. Lieutenant Gordon of the 93rd Highlanders, stationed in Halifax, planted the heather in 1838. He had it brought from Loch

Lomond and remained in the garrison long enough to see it take to its new home and spread.

The following theory is the most commonly accepted. Palliasses, or mattresses, used by the soldiers or by Scottish seamen, were filled with heather before they left Scotland and were eventually emptied near the shore. Halifax historian Lou Collins supports this theory.

Several Scottish regiments have been encamped in Point Pleasant over the years, the earliest of them in full Highland dress of belted plaid, the predecessor of the kilt. The belted plaid was a useful garment that could also serve as a blanket. (It had been proposed that their form of dress be changed to breeches for the Nova Scotia winter, but their leaders found that the men in Highland dress proved much healthier, even in North Atlantic gales, than the soldiers in more conventional uniforms. Marching through the rough tracks of Point Pleasant, they must have looked quite at home.)

It seems probable that sprigs of heather, even with roots attached, might have accompanied them, for it had many uses in their native land. There, heather provided brooms, pot scrubbers, bedding for animals and sometimes humans, it was used to make a primitive thatch, and, as heather flourished over large areas, it was readily available.

Point Pleasant Park supplied a friendly environment for the plant, which has flourished and spread. Park records of 1934 mention transplanting heather to other areas of the Park, and in the same year $1.30 was spent on heather seed.

John Buchan, author of stirring novels, many about Scotland, became Lord Tweedsmuir and governor general of Canada in 1935. Until the Tweedsmuirs left in 1940, the mayor of Halifax annually sent a bunch of Point Pleasant Park heather to Lady Tweedsmuir, no doubt to remind her of her native heath and make her feel at home.

The heather now covers a fairly widespread area of the Park. Many a Scottish immigrant still smiles at the sight of the familiar purple haze that heralds the coming of autumn, undoubtedly the most colourful season of the Park's year.

People admire the heather. (Castle)

Meeting in the heather (Ruth Kimmins)

Examples of 78th Highlanders' uniform 1869. Top, drummer and below, colour sergeant (Citadel)

9

The Point Pleasant Park Commission

May 7, 1866, marked the establishment, as a body politic, of the Directors of Point Pleasant Park, who would apply for licence from Her Majesty Queen Victoria's Principal Secretary of State for the War Department to "enter upon and occupy" the land as a park. Originally there were seven prominent citizens appointed as directors, plus the mayor and recorder of the City of Halifax. Sir William Young was the chosen president.

A new act in April 1873 once more incorporated directors of Point Pleasant Park—this time four citizens, including two of the original members, plus the mayor and one alderman from each ward in the city—to be elected annually by City Council. Sir William Young continued as president, or chairman. Secretary was Alderman John S. D. Thompson (future attorney-general of Nova Scotia, minister of justice, and prime minister of Canada). He had urged more speedy arrangements for the Park to be made ready for the public.

The directors took a keen interest in the laying out of the grounds and supervised closely. Daily walks were the usual routine for the four permanent members of the board. Sir William Young was especially involved. He expended both his energy and his own funds to make sure that work proceeded without more delays.

Sir William Young 1799–1887 (PANS)

Be it enacted by the Governor, Council, and Assembly, as follows :

Incorporation.

1. The Honorable William Young, James A. Moren, William Cunard, Andrew M. Uniacke, William J. Stairs, John Tobin, and John Doull, Esquires, and their successors, with the Mayor and Recorder of the City, are hereby constituted a body politic and corporate by the name of the *Directors of the Point Pleasant Park*, with power, in case of the death, incapacity, removal from the Province, or resignation of any one or more of the seven directors first named, to fill up such vacancies from time to time by new appointments, to be entered on their minutes.

Establishment of the Park Directors as a "body politic," 1866 (P. P. P. Records)

In 1893, in the annual report to City Council by John Doull, chairman, who succeeded Sir William Young, and George Lawson, secretary, the following statement was made [at right]:

The next year, the annual report echoed the previous dissatisfaction with the park budget: "At the close of the financial year on 1st April, the park account will have been overdrawn by necessary expenditure to the extent of two hundred dollars." Two years later, the annual report ends with a very brief summary of work accomplished and the phrase, "with the funds at our disposal."

Minutes were taken during meetings of the directors of Point Pleasant Park, or the Point Pleasant Park Commission. The first minute book, in use for nearly fifty years, was subsequently lost and few records of early meetings remain. In an address to the Commercial Club in 1920, Commission Chairman Hector McInnes, holding the minute book while he spoke, said that records until 1877 were in the handwriting of the late Sir John S. Thompson. Until 1920 there had been seven chairmen of the Commission, including himself. Following Sir William Young came John Doull, Hon. W. J. Stairs, Hon. William Chisholm, George C. Campbell and C. C. Blackadar. The current mayor acted as vice-chairman. Composed

Last spring about a thousand yards of new fencing was put up from waste material chopped in the process of thinning. This fencing was necessary in order to enclose the piece of ground belonging to the Imperial Government, which lies between the Park land and Mrs. Bauld's property. A dangerous part of Steele's pond was also fenced.

The Commissioners would further represent to the City Council that the present appropriation is insufficient to carry on the necessary work in maintaining so extensive an area of ground in a condition creditable to the city. An annual sum of at least $3000 should be placed at disposal of the commissioners.

The erection of a proper dwelling house for the park-keeper should also be provided for, as this has become a necessity, and cannot longer be delayed.

The accounts of expenditure by the commission from 1st April to 31st December, 1893, are submitted herewith, showing a balance due by the city of $224.31. A considerable expenditure will still have to be made before 1st April, 1894, which terminates the Park year.

JOHN DOULL, *Chairman*,
GEORGE LAWSON, *Secretary.*

(P. P. P. Records)

At the close of the financial year on 1st April, the Park account will have been overdrawn by necessary expenditure to the extent of $200.

JOHN DOULL,
Chairman of Commissioners.

GEORGE LAWSON, *Secretary.*

(P. P. P. Records)

106

Office of the City Clerk,

Halifax, N.S.

L. Fred Monaghan,
City Clerk.

January 17th 19 2

Hector McInnes, Esq.,

Bedford Row.

Sir:-

I have made, unavailingly, every effort to locate the Minute Book of Point Pleasant Park Commission. The best information I can get is that Mr. W.A. Black has it. He is now out of the City but is expected to return on Saturday, 20th inst.

Yours respectfully,

L. Fred Monaghan,

CITY CLERK.

CH.

(PANS)

of six Commission-appointed members and seven aldermen, the Commission made all decisions in running the Park, hiring the workforce and spending the budget.

A 1921 report mentions that the Commission consisted of six aldermen and four others. The chairman was to be elected annually. Meetings were usually held on Saturday mornings. In March 1955, because monthly meetings no longer seemed to be working

satisfactorily, the decision was made to call meetings at the discretion of the chairman.

Although numbers and methods of election varied for years, eventually the procedure was settled. In 1963, the system was set out in an act to *Amend and Consolidate Chapter 86 of the Acts of 1866, an Act to Incorporate the Directors of a Park at Point Pleasant, Halifax, Nova Scotia*. The directors of Point Pleasant Park were to continue to be a body corporate

under the name Directors of Point Pleasant Park. They should consist of eleven members (formerly nine in 1960). The four permanent commissioners had the right to appoint a new member if any vacancy occurred in their number. Usually they would choose someone already on the Commission. Three city taxpayers and three aldermen, (reduced to one in 1969), were to be appointed by City Council. The mayor completed the number. No time limit held for permanent commissioners, most of whom by this time had originally been city appointees. From that group normally came the chairman and vice-chairman, elected annually. It soon became customary for the officers to remain for a number of years and annual elections ceased. The city clerk was official secretary and took minutes. The city treasurer, later replaced by a member of the Commission, acted as treasurer. More people applied to join this board than any other in the city. In its last years, when many informal extra meetings were held, usually in the park restaurant, a member of the Commission was elected secretary to take over some of the city clerk's duties. At the formal meetings, held at City Hall, a secretary from the city clerk's office took minutes.

Park directors have been chosen from many different professions over the years. Several were lawyers, some were businessmen or

January 17th
1 9 2 3

Dear Mr. Mackinlay,-

    Mr. Hugh E. MacNab, the former secretary of the
Park Commission, has given me the minute book. It
follows that the minutes for the past year have been
kept on "scraps of paper". Neither of us want to
sit on a commission where the minutes are in such an
unsatisfactory state, and if you do not mind, you might
get together all the minutes you have and I can get from
the City Clerk the notes that he has, so that we may
arrange to have the minutes written up.

    Perhaps Thursday (tomorrow) you can drop into the
office with your material shortly before you go to lunch
and we can arrange to have the minutes engrossed satisfactorily on the book.

                     Yours very truly,

C. H. Mackinlay, Esq.,

    Messrs. A. & W. Mackinlay,

        City.

Then what happened to the minutes? They have not reappeared. (PANS)

Top, the Hon. H. P. MacKeen

Below, Alice MacKeen (Mrs. Judy Moreira)

engineers, two were lieutenant-governors of the province—Hon. H. P. MacKeen after and Hon. A. R. Abraham before their respective terms in office. On Hon. H. P. MacKeen's death in 1971, his wife, Alice MacKeen, became the first woman appointed to the board. She served for five years. It was common for permanent commissioners to serve long terms; some remained in office for more than twenty years.

The park superintendent controlled the day by day running of the Park and supervised the workforce. He worked very closely with the Commission, latterly attending all of

Bennett's Barriers

Top, Gordon Smith (Courtesy of The Halifax Herald Ltd.)

Below, G. Frank Bennett (G. Frank Bennett)

the meetings. In earlier times, he sent a written report.

In 1893, the city grant to the Park was $2,500, from which the park workers were paid, roads were kept up, the lodge keeper's and ferryman's houses were maintained. A century later, the budget, most of which was for wages, had increased to $152,879. The longtime chairman of the Commission, Gordon Smith, reported proudly that, in the previous year, a surplus balance of $6,500 had been shown and that the Park had operated within its budget for more than thirty years. During the last years of the Commission, the treasurer, Peter Herschorn, presented a budget of more than $400,000. Occasionally, special projects, such as major repairs to the park lodge in 1986, required additional funding to the normal budgetary

requirements. In such cases, the Commission would make a request to City Council, possibly appearing before it, to justify the expenditure.

The chairman following Gordon Smith was G. Frank Bennett. One of his innovations, laughingly called "Bennett's Barriers" by the other commissioners, are woven wooden screens that hide the entrances to the toilet facilities throughout the Park. Among recommendations when he gave up his appointment, Frank Bennett suggested that the chairman's term of office should be limited and also urged that individual members of the Commission should have more direct responsibilities. The latter came about, with fewer duties falling to the chairman.

Elliott Spafford, who followed Mr. Bennett, proposed that the terms of

The final three Park Commission chairmen, left to right: Elliott Spafford (Elliott Spafford), Janet Kitz (Ann Kitz) and Robert Weld, last Commission chairman (Robert Weld)

office for chairman and vice-chairman be a maximum of 2 two-year terms. The bylaws were adjusted accordingly. Janet Kitz, next chairman, was the only woman to hold the office. She was succeeded by Robert Weld, the last chairman and the one who served the shortest term—less than a year.

In April 1996, metro amalgamation brought the administration of the Park under the Halifax Regional Municipality's control. The Point Pleasant Park Commission came to an end.

10
Paying the Rent

To be paid by the Directors of Point Pleasant Park to the British Crown, Her Majesty Queen Victoria at the time of the original 999-year park lease, is the sum of one shilling, the annual rent for the park lands.

In the early days, the treasurer of the Commission simply paid the shilling and received a receipt. Payment was made in June as the act to appoint the directors was signed in May. With the passing years, the shilling was replaced by a quarter, its nearest Canadian equivalent in size and close enough in value.

As with all imperial properties, the Park had to be closed one day a year to maintain the Crown's right to the land. This custom ended after the Park was transferred to the Department of Northern Affairs in 1964. For many years an annual park inspection was held, often on the day the Park was closed, allow-

Both sides of the 1866 shilling (Kitz)

ing more scope for the procession. Local dignitaries were invited to drive round the perimeter, initially in horse-drawn carriages of various descriptions and later in cars. Usually there was a reception afterwards, at the home of one of the commissioners.

In 1963, the suggestion was made that the rent might be paid with more formality and that a

shilling rather than a mundane quarter should once more be the coin presented. The Commission decided that, in time for the hundredth anniversary of the founding of Point Pleasant Park, a Shilling Ceremony would be held before the annual inspection. In 1964, for the first time, the shilling was paid before the park tour on June 25, and a reception followed

111

MG 100 vol. 156 #27D

F & T 50,000 4—73 63/Gsɔ. No./230

W. O. Form 1452 B.

£ — " 1 " —

Halifax NS

13 June 1878

RECEIVED from *Directors Point Pleasant Park*

the Sum of _____ Pounds,

one Shillings, and *Rent to* Pence, as per Bill annexed.

46 to 31st March 1878.

Witness to Payment,

A.H.M Gardner Capta
Paymaster.

Receipt for one shilling paid as rent in 1878. (PANS)

Below, Constable Joseph Power, 1970 (R. Grantham, Halifax Police Department Archives)

at the home of the Hon. H. P. MacKeen, one of the directors.

To commemorate the centenary of the Point Pleasant Park Commission in 1966, a fountain was constructed at the Young Avenue entrance to the Park. It exemplified the versatility of the staff, particularly that of superintendent Jim Nickerson, who designed the fountain. No outside labour was used, apart from the mechanical equipment from Industrial Suppliers in Dartmouth, and the cost was kept to well under five thousand dollars.

On July 5, 1966, the hundredth birthday was celebrated. The shilling rent was paid to Dr. Stanley Haidasz, parliamentary secretary to the Minister for Northern Affairs. A tour of the Park followed, ending at the new fountain. Mayor Charles Vaughan complimented the Park Commission, especially chairman Gordon Smith, who devoted most of his life to his voluntary duties. The park superintendent and staff were commended for their dedication, and the mounted policemen and fire department for their contribution to park safety. Mayor Vaughan then pulled the switch, and jets of water rose high into the air to the crowd's warmly expressed admiration. Dr. Haidasz unveiled the plaque commemorating the hundredth anniversary of the Point Pleasant Park Commission. In 1967, the Shilling Ceremony coincided with the opening to the public of the renovated Martello Tower.

After the shilling had been formally paid to the regional director for the Department of Indian Affairs and Northern Development

Plaque at Centennial Fountain.

Plaque acknowledges Maj. Gen. K. C. Appleyard's contribution to the Park. (Castle)

The Centennial Fountain at the Young Avenue park entrance (Castle)

in July 1968, Mayor Allan O'Brien unveiled the plaque to General K. C. Appleyard, who had donated the Glasgow lamp standards that stand at the Tower Road entrance.

At the 117th payment of rent on July 5, 1983, Commission Chairman Frank Bennett displayed the silver cup originally presented to Major General Montague in 1875 in gratitude for the work that the soldiers under his command had performed in "laying out and beautifying" Point Pleasant Park. A letter had been received in 1977 from an antique dealer in Norfolk, England, stating that the trophy had come into his hands. Commission member Hector Porter bought the cup because of its significance to Point Pleasant Park and presented it to the Commission at their meeting on November 8, 1977. On July fifth

The present whereabouts of the Montague Cup are unknown. (Courtesy of The Halifax Herald Ltd.)

The Shilling Ceremony gave the opportunity to celebrate other special occasions. (P. P. P. Records)

at the Shilling Ceremony, 108 years after it was first awarded, Mr. Porter formally presented the cup to Mayor Ronald Wallace as a gift to the City of Halifax. Considerable applause followed, and the trophy received many admiring comments. Senator Henry Hicks came forward to accept the year's rent.

The United Kingdom changed its currency in 1985, and the shilling became obsolete. B. G. Smith, director of finance for the City of Halifax, suggested that it might be wise to collect a supply of shillings for future use. He contributed four. People sent donations of shillings so that the proper coin could continue to be used. Another came from Wales and two, obtained during World War 2 when the donor was a serviceman, from Kentucky.

At the 1985 ceremony, a Parks Canada representative presented Chairman Frank Bennett with a plaque in recognition of the Commission's contribution to conservation. The motorcade of commissioners, dignitaries and guests then proceeded around the outer road to the park restaurant, where the reception was held.

The Shilling Ceremony has continued over the years. It offers the opportunity for the Commission chairman to give an annual report on the state of the Park and the year's events. Specially invited guests, usually the mayor and a member of the federal government or the lieutenant-governor, have also been invited to give an address. The ceremony has been held at various sites, including beside the Martello Tower, at the Tower Road parking lot, and at the lower pavilion. Only once has the event been held on a Saturday—July 16, 1994—to coincide with National Parks Day.

In 1987, chairman Elliott Spafford noted that the six members of the park staff had a combined total of 114 years of continuous employment. He also commented on the annual fine weather that had attended the event. He attributed such good fortune to the continuing influence that previous chairman Frank Bennett had exerted on the weatherman during his six years in office. The sun continued to co-operate throughout Mr. Spafford's four-year term as chairman.

The 1992 Shilling Ceremony, when Janet Kitz had succeeded Mr. Spafford, was the one time that it rained. Hurriedly, arrangements were made to change the venue to the park restaurant. Unfortunately, the change in the weather coincided with the only occasion on which a military band had been engaged. The rain caused its cancellation, but two bandsmen who had not been informed agreed to take part. "God Save the Queen" and "O Canada" were sung to the accompaniment of two tubas.

A piper is always present at the ceremony, as well as two sentries in 78th Highland regiment uniform. All look very much in keeping with their surroundings. The mounted summer police patrol, both horses and riders—only one police officer and horse team in recent years—are popular guests. In 1993, Prince, the old horse, was given a standing ovation. In 1994, the new police horse was introduced. Upon Prince's death, the Halifax police department announced that it could not afford a new horse. The firm Burns, Fry, Ltd. came to the rescue, providing $40,653 for four years' upkeep of the service. Justice

Above, true to park tradition, bagpipes and Highland uniforms play an important part in the Shilling Ceremony. (Kitz)

Marching to the Shilling Ceremony (Frank Bennett)

An invitation (P. P. P. Records)

Bill Crowell (Kitz)

Prince and rider (Kitz)

Protector, the handsome new horse, and his rider were welcomed warmly by the assembled crowd.

On two occasions, Bill Crowell, a teacher from Liverpool, played his saxophone to accompany the national anthems. His payment was a shilling. Presentations of mounted, suitably engraved shillings have also been made to retiring, long-serving staff members. In 1993, Edgar Boutilier, foreman, (the second generation of his family to spend his working life in the Park), and in 1994, Gerald Bond, who succeeded him as foreman, were both honoured at the annual ceremony.

In 1995, Chairman Robert Weld spoke of the G7 and the staff's efforts to make the Park look as spruce as possible for potential visits by the eight assembled heads of government.

The Halifax Defence Complex of the Canadian Parks Service has been responsible for much of the organization of formalities and personnel. Shilling Ceremony receptions usually took place in the park restaurant, following the formal proceedings, and were by invitation only. For the last few years, much simplified versions have been held on site, with everyone welcome. The tour of inspection has been omitted.

The shilling has been paid to different authorities. Until 1906, it was presented to the British commander of the troops stationed in the Park. When the Canadian Department of Militia and Defence

Edgar Boutilier receives a shilling upon his retirement. (Kitz)

Lieutenant-Governor James Kinley addressed the Shilling Ceremony 1995. Seated from left are Peter Herschorn, Park Commission vice-chairman, Her Honour Mrs. Kinley and Commission chairman Robert Weld. (Castle)

formally took over, it also became the recipient of the shilling. Since 1964, the rent has been paid first to an official of the Department of Northern Affairs and Development, later to the local MLA and, more recently, to the lieutenant-governor of Nova Scotia. The lease-holder was still the Point Pleasant Park Commission.

A Victorian shilling, mounted in a transparent block, is used as the ceremonial token and is returned to be used again, but a more common shilling of later date is retained by the recipient as the year's fee for the continued use of the lands of Point Pleasant that serve as a well-loved public park.

Bob Weld was the last Commission chairman to conduct the ceremonies. The following spring brought metro amalgamation, and the end of the Point Pleasant Park Commission. The Point Pleasant Park Advisory Committee with the Canadian Parks Service and city staff continue the custom of paying the rent.

Chairman Janet Kitz presented this shilling, the annual rent for use of the waterfront park, to Lieutenant-Governor James Kinley on July 16, 1994. (Sandor Fizli photo, *The Sunday Daily News*, July 17, 1994)

11

The Superintendent's Lodge

Included in the lease for the Park was the use of the cable house on Pleasant Street at a nominal rent. Samuel Venner, the first superintendent, moved there in 1879. The chairman of the Point Pleasant Park Commission, in his 1893 annual report to City Council, stated, "The erection of a proper dwelling house for the park-keeper should also be provided for, as this has become a necessity and can no longer be delayed." A year later the cable house was described as being "not only insufficient but in a faulty sanitary condition." After fully considering the matter, the commissioners concluded that "a neat brick cottage at the gateway of Young Avenue would form a suitable and convenient lodge and would greatly improve the aspect of the park entrance." Funds for the project were requested from City Council.

By 1896, it had been decided that the lodge should be an exact

The cable house at the south end of Pleasant Street / Greenbank circa 1890 (PANS)

replica of the one at the entrance to Hughenden in England, the residence of the late Lord Beaconsfield, who, before being ennobled, was Benjamin Disraeli, Prime Minister of Britain. He died in 1881. Tenders were called for during 1896, and architects from the firm J. C.

Dumaresq were chosen. Building would be done by S. M. Brookfield. The sum of three thousand dollars would be borrowed to cover the costs. In the same year, the city was asked to pass a resolution appropriating five hundred dollars annually for six years towards repayment of

GATEHOUSE
POINT PLEASANT PARK
J.C. DUMARESQ c 1880
Sydney Dumaresq 1992

Right, (Sydney Dumaresq)

Below, the Lodge in winter (PANS)

Keeper's Lodge, (Winter)
Point Pleasant Park, Halifax, N. S.

the loan. The actual cost was closer to thirty-five hundred dollars. The lodge was ready for occupation in 1897. Samuel Venner was the first tenant and lived there until his death in 1906. He was followed by John Kline.

Superintendent Kline's report to the Commission in 1917 stated that the lodge was "a building entirely lacking in modern conveniences." At the end of that same year, it suffered three hundred dollars worth of damage caused by the Halifax Explosion. Plumbing was eventually improved, and in February 1925, the house was wired for electric light. Superintendent Kline would pay for his own light costs but not for the wiring.

In June 1930, John Kline died, and Thomas Fripps, the new superintendent, with his wife and daughter, moved into the lodge. He had use of the lodge with the added service of a telephone. Thomas Fripps was very familiar with Point Pleasant Park. His father had been park constable, and their home was nearby, on Pleasant Street, where he was born in 1888. When he joined the army in 1908, he was posted to the Park. He served overseas during World War 1. After his return in 1919, he lived in Point Pleasant Battery and then in Fort Ogilvie with his family. For the three years prior to becoming superintendent, he

120

The lodge 1904 (PANS)

The extension to the lodge, completed in 1950 (Castle)

had been in charge of the park subdistrict forts.

In October 1930, blasting for the new pier caused broken windows, shattered plaster and other damage to the lodge. A letter from the city clerk on behalf of the Park Commis-sion to the port authorities re-quested that blasting be made lighter and the damage repaired.

In July 1948, stone was removed from Cambridge Battery to build an addition to the lodge—the fort and lodge had been built of the same material. Work began in September 1950, and by December 1 the extension was completed.

After thirty years of living in the lodge and taking only one vacation, Thomas Fripps retired in December 1959.

The new superintendent, James (Jim) Nickerson, moved in. Like his predecessor, he had a long-standing connection with the Park. He was born a block away, on Tower Road. On his return from World War 2, he took up employment in the Park, becoming foreman in 1952 and superintendent in 1959. He lived in the lodge for more than two dec-ades, until 1980.

James Grant followed Jim Nickerson as superintendent, but

Tom Fripps with his tree nursery
(Muriel Griswold)

Below, fawns found in the Park in spring 1945. Mrs. Fripps bottle fed them and they became used to the Fripps' dogs.
(Muriel Griswold)

The fawns could scarcely walk.
(Muriel Griswold)

only for three years. On his departure owing to ill health, Loring (Hap) Sawler took over.

Hap Sawler had worked in the Park for over twenty years, travelling from St. Margaret's Bay. As he did not wish to move into the lodge, the Commission saw an opportunity to survey the building and undertake necessary restoration work.

A firm of architectural consultants was employed to make a detailed investigation of the lodge and to offer solutions to the various problems. Extensive exterior and interior renovations were proposed.

The interior was gutted, the basement filled with crushed rock, the main floor laid with concrete

Superintendent James
Nickerson (Jim Clark)

slab, new plumbing, wiring and
appliances provided, and the house
completely redecorated. The
exterior also required considerable
work due to leaks. Problems with
the lodge were not completely
solved. Leaks continued to be a
serious concern. Further work was
carried out in later years.

In December 1987, the park
foreman, Arthur Sampson, moved in
with his family. He became superintendent in the summer of 1988.
Since amalgamation of various
municipal authorities took place in
1996, the lodge has not been
occupied. The building remains as a
reminder of the superintendents
who made it their home.

12
People

Many people have called Point Pleasant Park home for differing lengths of time. The Mi'kmaq camped here with ready access to water routes and hunting. The earliest European settlers quickly moved further inland seeking a more sheltered location. The forts have housed varying numbers of soldiers, depending on threat of attack from the sea. During times of peace, when very limited staffs were considered necessary, some of the housing served as married quarters. A large artillery encampment in 1885 [illustrated on page 26–27] provided temporary accommodation. The tramp of soldiers, singly and in formation, was a common sound throughout the years. Even now, military trainees can be seen and heard marching through the main paths, often chanting as they step in rhythm.

Lord Dalhousie, in his journals edited by Marjorie Whitelaw, mentions Point Pleasant several times. In 1816, the earl was appointed lieutenant-governor of Nova Scotia. On November 11, 1816, he wrote: "I ordered the *Forth* to be saluted by all the Batteries as she passed in succession, and I rode out to Point Pleasant to see it. The scene was *Niger* here, & the spaniels round by Point Pleasant and the woods, skirting the Northwest Arm. No game or living thing to be seen except four old Indian native women, sitting like savages round a bit of fire, pictures of misery."

On May 1, 1817, he noted: "May Day is most delightful; by six o'clock the whole town almost was walking towards Point Pleasant gathering the mayflower all cheerful & gay. Welcome Spring with all its charms."

March 1819 must have produced unusual weather. On the second day of the month, he wrote: "A delightful summer day. I walked by the sea shore round Point Pleasant. Wet and

The Ninth Earl of Dalhousie, George Ramsay 1770–1838 (after the portrait by Sir John Watson Gordon) by Charles Fraser Comfort (Canada, b. 1900) (Dalhousie University Collection)

disagreeable underfoot, but the sun so warm that I sat down on the rocks nearly an hour, enjoying the heat of the day, and the fresh smell of seaweed on the beach."

On May 2, 1820, part of the entry reads: "This morning lady D. gave a breakfast in the woods at Point Pleasant to a large party of children, after having gathered their loads of Mayflowers; they have remained out till Evening & are come home delighted with their sport."

Other park users include the young Sir John S. Thompson, later involved in the Park's beginnings, who spent many leisure hours on the point or in the waters around it.

Joseph Howe was a frequent visitor, apart from his famous duel. He practised some of his more dramatic oratory here.

Throughout its existence as a park, Point Pleasant has provided miles of paths where people could

Far left, Muriel's grandfather William Fripps, born 1842, served as park constable. (Muriel Griswold)

Left, Tom Fripps served in the Royal Canadian Artillery in World War 1. (Muriel Griswold)

find peace to contemplate or compose, exercise or converse at length. In *Picturesque Canada*, a work issued in serial form by the Art Publishing Co. of Toronto about 1890 and described as "a beautiful specimen of Canadian art and Canadian workmanship," a romantic and complimentary description of the Park is included.

John W. Regan's book *Sketches and Traditions of the Northwest Arm* (1908), contains this description: "Its woodlands, driving roads and riding paths, twisting and twining with serpentine grace in and out through the forest of spruce and pine, with glimpses now of the harbor [sic] now of the Northwest Arm, anon of the broad ocean rolling in through the entrance of Chebucto Bay, and breaking on the beach at one's very feet, enchant the spectator."

In his book *To Nova Scotia*, published in 1935, T. Morris Longstreth describes his first visit to Point Pleasant Park, when his friend Dr. Weagle wished to "go sit by the water in the shade of a pine and read…." A taxi drove them to the Young Gates. After their walk, Dr. Weagle said, "This changes Halifax." Many people have had that feeling.

Muriel (Fripps) Griswold has a long association with Point Pleasant

Park. At the time she was born, her parents were living in Point Pleasant Battery. Her birth took place in the old Halifax Infirmary, but she returned to the fort as a newborn.

Her link with the Park goes back even further. Her grandfather served as park constable for many years. He lived first on Pleasant Street, where her father was born, and then Atlantic Street, just across from the Park. Her father, Thomas (Tom) Fripps joined the Royal Canadian Artillery, 9th Siege Battery. In 1908, he was posted to Point Pleasant Battery with his family. From 1914 to 1919, Tom Fripps served overseas. Unlike many of his comrades, he was lucky enough to escape serious injury over those long, dangerous years and return to his life in Point Pleasant Battery. In 1920, Muriel was born.

Muriel's earliest memories are of living in two separate wooden buildings, one containing the

Muriel with her uncle at Point Pleasant Battery in 1922 (Muriel Griswold)

kitchen and living room, the other, two bedrooms. When bedtime drew near, her mother would light a lantern to navigate the path from the back door to the bedroom. Windy, rainy nights were the worst, when a storm blew in from the Atlantic and waves crashed a few yards away.

Heat came from wood stoves, light from oil lamps. A lantern was necessary for a trip to the two-seater outhouse after dark. The well lay outside the fort, through the gate in the high metal fence that prevented public access, and across the road. The Fripps family made sure that they had fetched plenty of water for the household's needs well before nightfall on the long winter evenings. In part of the fort buildings, an

underground room, mounded up, made efficient cold storage for food, even in warm weather.

By the time Muriel started school, her family had moved to another stronghold in the Park, Fort Ogilvie. There they lived in a long building behind the huge, smooth rocks, where still visible are names and dates, cut into the stone by soldiers with plenty of time on their hands. The two large barrack rooms were occupied by soldiers, often stationed there for short terms, but Muriel was the only child in residence.

The fort was surrounded by a high stone wall, where large guns were mounted on the mound on the harbour side, giving cover to the harbour. If Muriel climbed up

beside the guns, she could see out over the ocean, as the trees were cut back to give a clear view for the gunners. Just outside the gate in the walls, apple trees grew and her father had planted a small garden. Her mother kept hens. Foxberries were plentiful in the woods just beyond, and Muriel would pick them for her mother to make pies and jam.

When she started at Tower Road School, Muriel found the way there and back on the wooded trails a bit long and lonely, as she usually walked by herself. She had a friend, Dorothy Neate, another army child, who lived in Point Pleasant Battery, but she took another path. However, they often took shortcuts through the woods between the

The rocks at Fort Ogilvie carved by soldiers with time on their hands. (Castle)

Fort Ogilvie gun emplacement 1977. Muriel Fripps saw the world from here as a child. (Jim Clark)

Muriel Fripps age eleven or twelve, Point Pleasant lodge (Muriel Griswold)

two forts to visit and play together. Other children at school, who lived in ordinary houses, were impressed when they learned where Muriel and Dorothy lived and liked to be invited to play with them.

In 1929, when Thomas Fripps was appointed park superintendent, the family moved to the park lodge. Muriel loved the new house. It was near the road, had more room, and was much handier to school. Soon,

she had transferred to College Street School and was given a bicycle, which made many places more easily accessible. She knew every path in the Park, secret places where berries or mushrooms could be found, strange-shaped trees and rocks. To her friends, the Park seemed like their own extended playground. The Quarry Pond, close to the lodge, offered skating in winter, polliwogs in spring, followed by frogs and minnows. Steele's Pond, even better for skating, was not as close. When the ice was good, it could be quite crowded. In the Park were sleigh rides, snowshoe clubs and all sorts of organized winter activities. In summer Black Rock Beach was a great place for swimming.

[Text continues on page 132.]

Below and right, Muriel
Fripps (Muriel Griswold)

Far right, Mr. and Mrs.
Tom Fripps (Muriel
Griswold)

Bottom, winter in the
Park (Mary Primrose)

Left, Tom Fripps (Muriel Griswold)

Left below, Elizabeth Fripps (Muriel Griswold)

Below, the park lodge and superintendent Tom Fripps (Muriel Griswold)

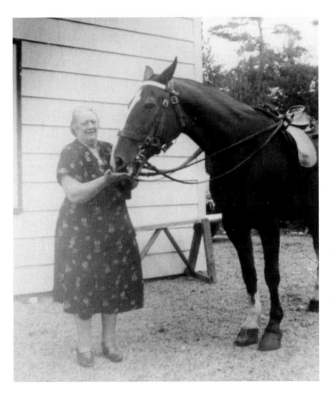

Right, the gravelly Black Rock Beach of Muriel Fripps' childhood (Anthony Lugar, Bauld Collection)

Below, the lodge garden (Muriel Griswold)

bottles and jars to many of the homes in the neighbourhood.

Some areas of the Park looked different when Muriel was a child. Black Rock Beach had no sand, just pebbles. Trees grew along the shore, the view across the water visible only from certain vantage points. Closer to the shore the ground was inclined to be marshy except in very dry summers. The forts came under military authority, and although not all were fully operational, soldiers and vehicles were a common sight. Walkers rarely ventured too near the surrounding walls and fences.

Muriel was married in the summer of 1941. The lodge garden, looking its best in brilliant sunshine, was the scene of her wedding reception, a fitting farewell to her life in the Park.

Grace (Neate) Molineux, daughter of Thomas William Neate of the Royal Canadian Artillery, was born in 1928, in one of the bedrooms in

Muriel used to cycle to the Royal Nova Scotia Yacht Squadron, near Black Rock Beach, and collect their scraps to help to feed her mother's hens. Eventually she went to the Convent of the Sacred Heart School and cycled every day.

During blueberry season, Muriel and her mother would take a trip by Purcell's ferry across the Arm, where the berries were plentiful. Blackberries grew in abundance in Francklyn Park, adjoining Point Pleasant. The lodge garden provided a good supply of soft fruit and vegetables. Mrs. Fripps made quantities of preserves and wine. At Christmas Muriel had the task of delivering

Above, Dorothy and Grace Neate
(Grace Molineux)

Right, Grace (Neate) Molineux stands
in the place where she was born.
(Castle)

Bottom, Grace and Muriel reunited at
Point Pleasant Battery. (Castle)

Point Pleasant Battery, where her father was stationed. She lived there until she was three years old with her parents and older sister, Dorothy, who was a great friend of Muriel Fripps. (Muriel and Dorothy went to the same school.)

Grace recalls one alarming event at the fort that occurred when her parents and friends went off for a brief sail. Unfortunately, the wind dropped, they were becalmed and did not return until four in the morning. Dorothy, left for what was meant to be a very short time, did not like to leave her sister to find help and was in a considerable state of worry by the time her parents finally reached home. The hours spent alone in the bleak fort at the edge of the sea seemed endless.

One park tragedy Grace remembers is that just down from Fort Ogilvie, a soldier hanged himself during the time her family lived in the battery. The children avoided that spot forever afterwards.

Gladys Eleanor Neate, Grace and Dorothy's mother, would walk from the battery into South End Halifax to shop, but newspapers were delivered to the forts. The boy who delivered them, James

Wilfred Creighton with his sister in the Park (Dr. W. G. Creighton)

Dr. Creighton at the Park in 1997 (Castle)

Nickerson, eventually became park superintendent.

The Neate and Fripps parents played cribbage together by lamplight in the evenings while the Fripps lived at Fort Ogilvie then, briefly, the lodge. There was considerable social life in the Park among the families who lived there, at the forts and the Purcell's house. Evenings ended with long walks home in the dark.

In 1931, Thomas Neate was moved to the South Barracks.

Although they no longer lived in the Park, the Neate family remained frequent visitors.

Dr. Wilfred Creighton has been familiar with Point Pleasant Park for years. Born in 1904, he lived with his family on Oakland Road, very handy for exercising his mother's mare in the Park. When old enough, he drove in the buggy drawn by the lively horse, sticking to the outer road. All three forts were occupied by troops with limited married quarters.

As a boy, Wilfred Creighton enjoyed driving by Point Pleasant Battery where the resident family had several dogs that barked furiously from inside the high fence at the sound of the horse's hooves. At that time, the area between the main road and the sea was mainly swampy or treed, except where trees had been cut to allow clear views for the forts' gunners. He used to bicycle down to Chain Rock to play, or even swim and picnic.

When he grew up, Wilfred Creighton studied forestry, both in New Brunswick and Germany. He worked for the provincial forestry department, becoming chief provincial forester, and, later, deputy minister of Lands and Forests. In these roles, he visited and gave advice to the superintendent in Point Pleasant Park. A good, healthy mixed forest with hard- and softwoods was the aim.

David MacKeen's father, Hon. H. P. MacKeen, QC, and his mother, Mrs. Alice MacKeen, were members of the Point Pleasant Park Commission. The MacKeen family lived near the Park during the earlier part of David's life, and he spent a great deal of time at Point Pleasant.

He has a vivid memory of walking with his father on one of the last days of August 1939. Preparations were underway for the imminent war. Troops seemed to be everywhere. The gates to Fort Ogilvie had been closed, but the commanding officer,

a friend of his father, invited them to enter the fort. Soldiers oiled guns on the battlements, while others cut the tops off nearby trees to give a clear line of fire. Mr. MacKeen, who had served in the artillery during World War 1, suggested putting sandbags round the gun abutment for protection. The CO replied proudly that his men were not going to duck flying cement, and he would do no such thing.

At night, during wartime air raid drills, David recalls how the searchlight beams from Point Pleasant Battery shone and flickered over the water, making eerie patterns on the waves and sky. Troops banned entry into the forts through the war years. The ruined fortifications that were not in use, such as Chain Rock Battery, and the large flat rocks made ideal places to play. Some of the British evacuees who came to the Park were bewildered by a sign near the Miller Street entrance, which read, "Drink Canada Dry."

Left, Hon. H. P. MacKeen, QC, David's father (David MacKeen)

Right, David, his sister Judy and friend Christina with their second-hand wartime bicycles, an alternative to horses. (David MacKeen)

Among David's pleasant memories of the Park is playing ice hockey on the Quarry Pond. Opposing teams were made up of students from the two local schools, Tower Road and St. Francis, and David mentioned that the struggle often involved religion.

People commonly exercised their horses in the Park. Nearby was a stable with three mounts for rent to be ridden in the Park. Sometimes incompetent riders were thrown. Then the horses simply headed for home. David, galloping on one of these, was thrown and broke his thumb. After that incident his father bought a pony for safer riding.

Right, a trip with Bill Purcell was always a treat. (Carol Anne Janc)

Below, the empty Martello Tower was a great place to play. (PANS)

David's usual route followed the quieter side paths, where he often met no one; the interior of the Park was less frequented fifty years ago.

Purcell's ferry and the Purcell family are high on his list of happy memories. Bill Purcell was unbelievably good with children. Many summer trips were made on the power boat to Purcell's Cove, where there was a little store. There David tasted grapenut ice cream for the first time. Over half a century later, the memory of that wonderful flavour lingers. Berry-picking often followed a visit to the store, and then the return journey. The trip made a wonderful day out. Walks in Point Pleasant Park with his dog are still an enjoyable part of David MacKeen's life.

James Nickerson, Jr., known as Jimmy, is the son of James Nickerson who was superintendent of Point Pleasant Park from 1958 to 1980. The senior Nickerson worked in the Park soon after his return from war, and for a time the Nickersons lived in Fort Ogilvie's married quarters. (Two other families also lived there.)

Jimmy has very happy memories of that time. He was popular with the other boys at school. On his first day at a new school, students were asked their name and father's occupation. When Jimmy hesitated, another boy answered for him, "Everyone knows his father owns Point Pleasant Park."

The imagination of active boys living in a fort led to the most exciting games. Fort Ogilvie would be held by one group, the Canadians or even the British, while another group, usually the Germans soon after World War 2, tried to capture it. The battles were taken with some seriousness and different tactics were employed. At the movies, Jimmy and his friends saw a pit dug and covered with branches as a booby trap. It seemed an excellent idea. Unfortunately, his father

Above, Jimmy Nickerson today (Castle)

Below, superintendent Jim Nickerson after his retirement (Jim Nickerson)

Ronald (Ron) Grantham points out the rock hollowed out by a bank robber. There his loot was stored while he was in jail. This happened when Ron was a boy and he grew up to work as a Halifax police officer. (Castle)

received a complaint from an adult neighbour who had fallen into it, and pits were forbidden. The children built wigwams out of spruce boughs and knew every hollow rock and unusual formation in the Park.

Jimmy used to go out with Bill Purcell on trips, and once helped in the rescue of two boys whose outrigger canoe had swamped. Bill had to place the older boy on a board and force water out of him. Jimmy also remembers happier outings, such as when they watched a fireworks display. Cribbage matches are another pleasant memory—the game has always been a favourite at the Park.

When Jimmy was nine or ten, there was considerable commotion in the middle of the night. The police had followed a bank robber into the Park, where he trying to break open a safe. The next morning, Jimmy and his brother scoured the ground but found only a few pennies.

Winter was wonderful, with skating, tobogganing and even skiing on an old pair of second-hand skis. The hill leading down from the Martello Tower towards the Arm made an exciting ski run. A policeman on horseback might even give a tow back up.

The move to the park lodge pleased all the Nickerson family. It

Even with thousands of users, you can still find your own space in the Park. (Castle)

Below, (Castle)

was a quaint house with a wonderful setting. By that time, Jimmy's interests had widened, and he was happy to be nearer school and public transport.

Today, there are the daily users, most of whom arrive at a regular time and may even follow a particular route to walk, run, cycle or feed the resident birds and squirrels. Neither the season nor the weather is a deterrent for most of them. Often they are accompanied by a dog, possibly more than one. Conflicts occasionally arise, but tolerance usually prevails. Acquaintanceships, even friendships have been established in the Park. There is camaraderie, with greetings and snippets of conversation exchanged. Absence causes comment: "Are you well? Were you away?" One newcomer to the city wrote to the Commission that he

had been rather lonely until he discovered the Park and began daily walks there. He soon met people and now feels happily at home. He wished to say thank you

A recent survey, covering only two entrances on a sunny Sunday, made a count of 5,537 park visitors. Statistics from the Point Pleasant

Park Advisory Committee show that an estimated annual total would exceed 1 million. More than seventy per cent are walkers, almost half of that number accompanied by dogs. Runners and joggers make up twenty-five per cent, cyclists are much in the minority.

[Text continues on page 142.]

How many ways to enjoy the Park? As many as there are people to enjoy it. (Castle)

(Castle)

Roberta Bondar 1994 (Basil Grogono)

Among the well-known modern-day visitors is Roberta Bondar, astronaut and chair of the Friends of the Environment Foundation, on June 1, 1994. The foundation donated a gift of trees and shrubs to be planted in the Park. During the G7 Summit Conference in June 1995, US President Clinton, accompanied by several Secret Service agents, ran at fair speed, making a circuit from the entrance by the centennial fountain, along the waterfront and back by the steep Northwest Arm trail. Mrs.Aline Chrétien was seen walking in the Park during the same conference, and Mrs. Naina Yeltsina was given an official tour accompanied by superintendent Art Sampson.

There are many parks in the metro area, but regular users, some of whom travel many miles and bypass entrances to other beautiful walking places, regard only Point Pleasant as "The Park."

Superintendent Art Sampson accompanied Mrs. Naina Yeltsina on a tour of the Park. (Basil Grogono)

Richard Bernard, one of the park workers, was at his usual task of clearing up the untidiness of the previous day's visitors, when his attention was attracted by a small group of men running along the Shore Road. He looked more carefully. Was it possible? He had prayed the night before that he might see the president of the United States. Here he was. Richard approached the group and was allowed to shake Mr. Clinton's hand. (White House Photographic Services)

13

Monuments

Point Pleasant Park, situated at the mouth of Halifax Harbour, with sweeping views of the Atlantic Ocean, seems a natural place for naval monuments. Every ship entering or leaving port passes the park shore. People have watched silent sailing vessels, puffing steamships, modern highly powered container ships and glamorous cruise ships. Cargoes—human and freight—were once obvious. Now the huge containers hide their contents, and boatloads of immigrants standing at the rails are a sight of the past. Tugs and pilot boats, tiny beside the vast bulk of the large vessels, purposefully go about their duties, escorting and guiding. Oil tankers are more distant from the shore, the Dartmouth side their destination.

World Wars 1 and 2 produced the greatest volume of shipping. Then there came troopships, hospital ships, munitions ships, warships,

View from the Park past the Hen and Chickens Rocks and into the Atlantic (Castle)

freighters, some in convoys, others sailing alone. Shore guns were at the ready in case of hostile attack.

Memorials now remind park users of what happened at sea. The most imposing is the Sailors'

Monument that overlooks the ocean, the grave of those whose names appear on bronze panels mounted on the granite plinth. A "Cross of Sacrifice" rises high above. Floodlit at night, the

143

Right, container ship and tug
(Castle)

Below, two very different
vessels (Castle)

Bottom, wartime convoy (MCM)

structure acts as a lighthouse for modern mariners. Unveiled on Remembrance Day, November 11, 1967, the monument originally bore 3,267 names of those lost at sea in two world wars. The names are not only those of sailors. Troopships carrying soldiers and nurses were sunk. Many freighters landed in the ocean's depths. Names have been added to the plaques. Built by the Commonwealth War Graves Commission and the federal government, the Sailors' Monument "commemorates the officers and men of the Royal Canadian Navy, Canadian Army, and Merchant Marine of Canada and Newfoundland who in World Wars 1 and 2 went down to the sea in ships and never returned." These words were part of the address by the minister of Veterans Affairs at the official unveiling ceremony. Lieutenant-Governor H. P. MacKeen, a veteran of both world wars, drew the cords to pull back the maple leaf and Union Jack flags and reveal the plaques to the solemn crowd that

The Sailors' Monument (Castle)

The Seamen's Memorial at Point Pleasant Park (Thomas Raddall Collection, Dalhousie Archives)

The same memorial on Citadel Hill (Kitz)

stood beside the grey sea under a cloudy sky.

The Commonwealth War Graves Commission book that lists the names contains the following paragraph concerning the contribution of the Canadian Navy in the war at sea on the North Atlantic:

But the victory was not won without cost. Ships steaming without lights through fog, or storm, in the dark of a winter's night, vanished into the icy depths. Torpedoes and bombs took their toll. The quarter-deck lookout would be found to be missing from his station, the victim of a smashing sea. Engagements between opposing destroyers, frigate and submarine, coastal force and shore battery, resulted in the loss of ships and men. Sometimes a ship would limp into port bearing her dead for burial at shore, but, for the most part, the sailors of Canada who gave their lives found no grave but the sea.

The Seamen's Memorial, dedicated on August 10, 1924, had

The original plan for the Naval Monument. The Commission objected to the amount of land involved. (PANS)

The ceremonies (Castle)

NAVAL MONUMENT HALIFAX
PROPOSED DEVELOPMENT OF
THE BATTERY SITE

FOR THE I.W.G.C.

stood on the nearby headland. It recorded five hundred names of those killed in World War 1. In 1954, it was removed to Citadel Hill, refurbished, and World War 2 casualty names were added. By November 1966, vandalism, the weather and soil slippage from this site all contributed to a bad state of decay. The International War Graves Commission decided to build the new Sailors' Monument. The proposed location met with objections. The Park Commission was not keen on losing a number of fine trees. Some people felt that the monument would be more appropriate in a military setting or in the city. However, the original plans, which would have involved removing a summer house, new

parades of sailors and cadets march along the harbourfront road to attend, along with large crowds, a remembrance service. Poppies are conspicuous on caps and lapels. Although the service begins shortly before eleven o'clock, many arrive at the parking lot much earlier. The walk to the monument is slower for the World War 2 veterans, many supported by canes, who come to pay their respects to lost shipmates. "I was on three ships that went down," said one frail former member of the Merchant Navy. "I was lucky, but a lot of my mates weren't. I come every year, and I read their names."

The bugler sounds "The Last Post," and as the notes fade across the water, eyes and imaginations turn to the expanse of ocean. A more fitting place for such a ceremony would be hard to envisage. The monument can be seen by all ships entering or leaving the harbour. Wreaths are laid, and at the end of the service individuals leave their poppies tucked around the plaques.

Early in May, Battle of the Atlantic Sunday is commemorated at the Sailors' Monument. Judging by the long list of names of those who died in 1942, it must have been a particularly dangerous time to cross the Atlantic. May 1943 marked the end of the appalling losses. Improved weapons, aircraft and escort ships, along with the breaking of enemy secret codes caused the sinking of thirty-one German submarines that month. The last two years of World War 2 show far fewer names. The ceremony at the monument is laden with sadness at the loss of so many lives and thankfulness for the end of unremitting sea battles.

After a short religious ceremony and prayers, a bugler sounds "The Last Post," after which the attending chaplains read out the names of the ships that were lost. A two-minute silence follows, ended by the stirring

paths and extensive landscaping, were simplified and finally won general approval.

A year before the new Sailors' Monument was completed, just before Remembrance Day 1966, an unusual ceremony took place in the deepest part of Bedford Basin, where so many wartime ships had lain at anchor. The old Seamen's Memorial, broken up into four blocks, had been loaded on to a floating navy crane. Two naval chaplains conducted a service. Then, to the haunting sound of "The Last Post," the blocks were slipped into the waters of the Basin, officially buried at sea.

Twice a year, the tall Sailors' Monument in the Park is the focus of naval ceremonies. On November 11,

Right, the flagstaff and memorial
(Castle)

Below, inscription at the plaque near
the flagstaff (Castle)

THIS MAST IS DEDICATED TO THE MEMORY
OF THOSE VALIANT SHIPS, MEN & WOMEN WHO
FOUGHT THE CONVOYS THROUGH TO NORTH RUSSIA
AGAINST A FORMIDABLE AND DETERMINED FOE
DURING THE SECOND WORLD WAR

"Remember well to whom you owe your comfortable berth"

Dedicated by
The Atlantic Chief and
Petty Officers Association
and The North Russia Club
1998

notes of "The Rouse." Wreaths are laid at the monument and at sea.

Floodlights for the memorial were presented by the Royal Canadian Naval Association. It was first illuminated in May, 1969.

Not far from the Sailors' Monument, on top of a small rise overlooking the harbour entrance stands a monolith with an interesting inscription: "In Lasting Memory of Rear Admiral Walter Hose, C.B.E., R.C.N. 1875–1965. In adversity, neither politics, lack of money, nor ridicule could beat the determination and courage of this officer. This memorial was erected by the officers and men of the RCN and RCNR and dedicated the 2nd October, 1967 on the 92nd anniversary of the birth of Rear Admiral Hose. It is their tribute to a great and gallant sailor-warrior." A former British naval officer who resigned to join the RCN, he was recognized as father of the Royal Canadian Navy and founder of the Naval Reserve of Canada. He was the first chief of the naval staff.

The continuation of the Canadian navy was threatened by defence cuts in the early twenties and thirties. Rear Admiral Hose experienced serious difficulties in his ultimately successful efforts to ensure the future of the naval service.

In August 1973, an unusual monument, erected by the Naval Officers' Association, was dedicated by Admiral Timbrell. The chosen site was above the rocks on the shore where the searchlight had previously stood. This obsolete piece of

Above and right, Hose monument and its location (Castle)

Right, anchor of *Bonaventure* (Castle)

equipment was quickly demolished by the navy, which also took charge of construction of the memorial, with the exception of the steps that were built by park staff. Now the six-ton anchor and chain of HMCS *Bonaventure*, silhouetted against the ocean, form the background for the names of the Armed Forces of Canada members who lost their lives in peacetime, and for whom there is no known grave.

Nearby, the capture of the American ship *Chesapeake* by the British HMS *Shannon*, which triumphantly towed its captive into Halifax Harbour in June 1813, is celebrated. Surely on that occasion, the spectators on shore must have cheered the first British naval success after a series of defeats in single-ship engagements during the War of 1812.

At the wall beside Black Rock Beach, Sir Samuel Cunard is remembered. Born in Halifax in 1787, he founded a commercial empire in the Maritimes and played an integral part in developing Atlantic steam navigation. In July 1840, he inaugurated the Liverpool-Halifax-Boston mail service via the *Britannia* that, on every voyage, steamed past the site of the Cunard monument.

Facing the container piers rather than the ocean stands a special memorial to SS *Point Pleasant Park*. Soon after the freighter was

Right and below, HMS *Shannon* and the vanquished *Chesapeake*, the event (PANS) and its monument (Castle)

Bottom, Cunard monument (Castle)

launched in 1943 at Montreal, she came to Halifax for minor repairs to her engine. The ship and crew were accorded a civic welcome by Mayor John Lloyd, who presented a framed photograph of the Young Gates at the park entrance. It was to hang in an honoured place on board.

On February 23, 1945, the ship was sunk five hundred miles northwest of Capetown in the South Atlantic Ocean. Nine men were lost. The survivors sailed in lifeboats for ten days, covering 414 miles until their rescue by a South African ship.

Captain Paul Tooke, former third officer of SS *Point Pleasant Park*, began a successful effort in 1967 to erect a monument in the place that gave the ship its name. He later managed to identify the German submarine that had sunk the freighter and exchanged letters with the commander, who sent a wreath to be placed on the monument and expressed his deep regret at the

loss of men. He had been under the impression that all had survived. "May this monument play its part in letting former enemies become friends … and may it be a reminder for peace in this world of ours," he wrote. (Extra information is taken from an article by Alex Nickerson, *The Chronicle-Herald*, March 4, 1989.) The cairn is dedicated to the memory of "these gallant and unsung men of the Merchant Navy and to the happy ship in which they served Canada and died for her freedom…. The Southern Cross their eternal flame." The picture of the park entrance lies, with its namesake, at the bottom of a distant sea.

Trees have been planted for special occasions and in memory of six park commissioners, all serving members at the time of their respective deaths, including long-time chairman, Gordon Smith, and former lieutenant-governor

and commissioner, H. P. MacKeen. Near the Sailors' Monument, among the heather, are two plaques. One tells of twenty-five Canadian red maples planted to mark the Silver Jubilee of Queen Elizabeth in 1977. Only nine remain. The other commemorates the visit of the Queen Mother to Halifax in June 1979, but few signs of the special trees survive.

There are other unique memorials that mark personal contributions to the Park. The two pavilions, or summer houses, donated by William West, are inscribed with his name. A plaque on the Centennial Fountain at the Young Avenue entrance bears the inscription,

This fountain was erected to commemorate the 100th anniversary of the Directors of Point Pleasant Park, 1866–1966.
    Chairman G. E. Smith Esq.
    Hon. H. P. MacKeen, CD, QC
    Mayor C. A. Vaughan
    Alderman G. S. Black, QC
    Alderman J. L. Connolly
    R. A. Kanigsberg, QC
    Alderman R. A. O'Brien
    H. P. Briggs Esq.
    A. E. Johnson Esq.
    H. O. Mills Esq.

Around the Tower Road entrance parking lot stand five ornamental metal lamp standards, formerly owned by the Glasgow Corporation Lighting Department and dated 1910. They, along with three horse watering troughs, were donated to the City of Halifax by British industrialist General K. C. Appleyard, who had been instrumental in forming the province's Industrial Estates Ltd. and Halifax Developments, Ltd. After some controversy, with one member of the Commission, Robert Kanigsberg, strongly contesting their suitability, the Park Commission agreed to accept the lamp standards but refused the troughs.

When General Appleyard died in 1968, the industrial companies wished to erect a large granite tablet at the Tower Road entrance in his memory, but the Commission decided against it. Instead, a small metal plaque was mounted on one of the lamp standards.

At a Park Commission meeting, Mr. Robert Kanigsberg raised the question of the principle of permitting plaques to individuals. He feared that the Park would soon be filled with them. In later years the Commission decided to discourage the proliferation of memorials; however, the monuments add interest to a visit to Point Pleasant Park, encouraging the imagination to conjure the events linked with its history and surroundings.

Embossing on base of lamp standard (Castle)

The lamp standards (Castle)

14

The Park's Progress

In 1893, a report to the mayor and City Council, signed by John Doull, chairman, and George Lawson, secretary, was made on behalf of the Point Pleasant Park Commission. The tone reflected the members' feeling that the city had been less than generous with its grant. "With the limited means at its disposal" the Commission had not been able to enter upon any extensive scheme of improvement. Only such work had been carried out "necessary to preserve the natural beauties of the park, and its scenic and scientific features of interest, and to provide and keep in repair the necessary roadways, seats and other facilities, so that the citizens and summer visitors to the city may fully enjoy this pleasant retreat." The roads, footpaths and carriage drives had been kept in as fair condition as possible, but considerable extension and improvement were still necessary.

REPORT COMMISSIONERS POINT PLEASANT PARK.

———

HALIFAX, *December, 1893.*

To His Worship the Mayor and City Council of Halifax:

The Commissioners of Point Pleasant Park beg leave to submit to the Council their report upon the condition of the Park, and the work done during the year. With the limited means at disposal, it has not been possible to enter upon any extensive scheme of improvement. The commissioners feel that their chief duties are to carry out such work only as is necessary to preserve the natural

(P. P. P. Records)

Much labour was expended on forestry work, thinning, pruning and removing dead, dry timber because of fire hazard. The park nursery grounds had supplied healthy young trees as replacements, which had been purchased at little cost when very small and grew rapidly into "robust, valuable trees" with proper care. For future use, three thousand Norway spruce, one thousand Scotch fir or pine and four hundred hardwood trees of different kinds remained. About a thousand yards of fencing had been put up, made from waste material chopped in the process of thinning, and separated imperial government land from that of Mrs. Bauld, whose property was the closest to the Shore Road entrance to the Park

In 1894, the grounds had been cared for in the usual manner. Roads and paths had been remade

Park roads circa 1894 (PANS)

Branches were used for fencing and seats. These must have been some of the Commission's park-raised trees. (Gareth Harding)

Greenbank, Point Pleasant Park, Halifax, N.S.

or extended. About fifteen hundred healthy young trees were transplanted from the park nursery grounds to various areas. Some two thousand more had reached sufficient maturity to be moved in the spring. The commissioners had imported from Scotland one thousand Norway spruce, one thousand Scotch fir and five hundred elm, all seedlings, to the park nursery. More were to come the following spring to keep up the supply. Fifty new rustic seats were being constructed out of the material furnished by the tree trunks and branches that had been removed where necessary.

The 1894 report of the park commissioners reads: "In all the improvements and operations undertaken by the Commissioners, the greatest care is taken to preserve the natural features of the park scenery so far as compatible with the safety and convenience of the public and the requirements of the Military authorities." Samuel Venner, park superintendent at this time, carried out his duties to the satisfaction of the commissioners.

At the close of the financial year, the commission chairman, John Doull, concluded, the park account would be overdrawn by two hundred dollars, necessary expenditure. Reports continued to mention briefly forestry work and comment on limited finances.

Early in the 1900s, the Commission decided that paths should be named. Some names had already developed from common usage. Of proposals such as Harbour Road, Old French Road, Montague Road and even names of former Commission members, none

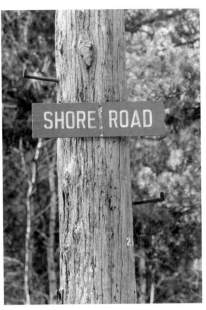

All signs were made by park staff. (Castle)

Superintendent Thomas Fripps (Muriel Griswold)

survive. Shore Road, Heather Road, Arm Road remain as before, with fort and tree names making up the others.

By 1912, 130 rustic seats had been placed in suitable spots for rest or picnics. A complaint that same year was that liquor was being obtained on Sundays from Cambridge Battery. The chairman of the Commission wrote a stiff letter to the officers commanding regarding the conduct of certain soldiers.

In 1914 came the suggestion that the Point Pleasant Park Commission also undertake the management of Fleming Park on the other side of the Arm. Members felt that would add too much to their duties and rejected the idea. A request that the Park should be used for a scout camp for the whole of the summer of 1915 was also refused. Already, military activities had increased because of the war,

and the Commission felt that enough land was restricted for public use.

That same year, Miss Daisy Thorne, who ran the tearoom, received permission to open on Sunday for the sale of tea, bread, and so on but no cigars or cigarettes. The Board of Control once again asked that the Commission manage Fleming Park but received another refusal.

For the next few years, requests were often made that cars be allowed to drive at least one way along the Shore Road. Always the answer remained the same: apart from necessary military or delivery vehicles, no cars would be permitted in Point Pleasant Park.

After the death of Superintendent Kline in 1930, Thomas Fripps was appointed in his place. With his wife and daughter, he moved into the lodge.

In April of the following year, one hundred three-foot grafted copper beech seedlings, plus fifty purple beech were received from a nursery in St. Catharines, Ontario. A year later, all driftwood removed from the waterfront was sent as fuel to the City Home. At times, the City Prison, too, used driftwood from the shore.

In the spring of 1934, thirty-seven hundred dead trees were cut and removed. Around the Martello

Open space was created around
Martello Tower. (PANS)

one in an enclosed area near the
lodge. See Superintendent T. W.
Fripps' report below and continued
on the next page.

During other years, Superintendent Fripps supplied the Halifax
Public Gardens and other city-
owned parks with surplus trees
from his nursery. In the spring of
1937, the park lodge nursery was
enlarged to hold about six thousand trees and some six hundred
Douglas fir were being reared in
the Cambridge area. Throughout

Tower and in various other places,
the ground was cleared, leaving
open, grassy spaces. Enough hay
was harvested to feed the park
horses, those at two hospitals and
some belonging to the tramway. A
hundred loads of wood were given
away, and eight thousand loads of
brush were taken to the beach and
burned. (A few unpleasant incidents
in the woods had made the superintendent and Commission, in
consultation with the police, decide
that too much underbrush provided
cover for undesirable elements.)
During the Depression, men employed under a relief programme
spent time in the Park, and their
labour speeded the general tidying
that was taking place.

Although new stock sometimes
came from other sources, most was
grown in park nurseries, the main

```
To the Chairman
        and
The Directors
of Pt. Pleasant Park.
    Halifax.N.S.

Gentlemen:-
        I beg to report on work performed at Pt.Pleasant Park.
            during the year 1935 —1936.

The breakwater was extended over 100 feet. it has been constructed of
heavy pine logs bolted together in sections and filled with stone.
Front of breakwater built up with heavy stone.
Repairs to old breakwater — 2 sections.
Seawalls were constructed along banks to save from washing away.
 Repairs to roads and footpaths were carried out
443 Loads of earth used on roads
128 Loads of beach gravel  Screened and used on roads
 80 Loads of earth used on bridle path.

TREES    700 trees which were in the nursery were transplanted to
         various parts of the Park and about 200 trees in the Park were
         transplanted in new locations.  3,000 new trees were placed in
         our Nursery,        Trees in Nursery
                                Cedar
                                Scotch  pine
                                White   pine
                                Red  _  pine
                                Sitka  spruce
                                Native  spruce
                                Copper beech
                                Chestnut  and Oaks

This year  The Provincial Forestry Department will send us 5,000
      young trees,  Scotch pine 2,000
                    Norway pine 1,000
                    Norway Spruce 1,000
                    Sitka Spruce  900
                        Cedar     100
                                5,000
```

Repairs to buildings

The old workshop on side of the barn has been removed and the ground cleaned up, also old coal shed was removed and the side of the shed shingled. A new concrete floor was laid in new workshop, also new windows placed and the necessary benches and racks installed. The building is now in a good condition.

A forty-five foot flag staff was placed in the centre of the new lawn bearing the Nova Scotian Flag.

A new fence was placed around the nursery and painted.

grass throughout the Park was cut (fodder for horse).

The guns at the Sailors Monument were repaired and painted.

Pruning dead branches from living trees

New permanent benches were put in the park and the old benches and tables repaired and painted.

The fence around the new lawn and Lodge was painted.

Fire places were build for the use of picnic parties

Heather transplanted to various places in the Park.

Respectfully Submitted
T.W.Fripps) Supt
Point Pleasant
                  Park

Working at one of the park nurseries
(P. P. P.)

Superintendent Fripps' 1916 report to the Park Commission (PANS)

the Park, four thousand trees were transplanted.

In 1936, there occurred several fires in the Park. The difficulty of obtaining water made the situation much more dangerous. Only by frequent patrolling was a serious outbreak averted.

In May 1937, the Department of National Defence decided to offer for sale three 9-inch guns that stood guard on the shore. The Commission wished them to remain because they were of interest to tourists and their removal might injure park roads. A year and a half later, soldiers pushed one gun over the steep bank into the sea, but two others were mounted on concrete pedestals, since no wheels proved available.

The much increased military activity during World War 2 caused considerable damage to roads and to the areas near the two forts—Fort Ogilvie and Point Pleasant Battery—that were in use. A fire, started at Point Pleasant Battery in mid-1945, destroyed more than two hundred trees. In November of that year, work was carried out by military parties to try to restore the Park to its pre-war condition.

After World War 2 ended, several ambitious plans were discussed by the Board of Works and the Park Commission. A zoo with native animals, hard surfaced roads,

Right, remounted gun
(Castle)

Below, Tom Fripps surveys
the damage after a major
storm in June 1953. (P. P. P.)

bathhouses, a lifeguard and a rescue boat were among the proposals, along with the plan to double the budget. Few of the ideas materialized.

In 1947, military authorities agreed to repair the damaged roads, as the earlier work had not achieved the desired results. In 1951, Commission Chairman Gordon Smith wrote to the local MP appealing for further help in the matter. That measure proved effective. Soon afterwards a sum of forty-five hundred dollars for road repairs was granted by the Department of National Defence.

It was then possible to spend money on the roads, but consensus about the materials to use was preceded by controversy. Should they be tarred? Were dirt roads more suitable? Crushed stone and binder dust? Cinders and ashes from school furnaces had been used during the previous century, but that solution was no longer possible. Finally, the Commission agreed: ash mixed with earth would be used. The work would be carried out by the park superintendent and staff.

In the early fifties, after the roads were improved, snow ploughing was begun for the first time but only after a very heavy snowfall, and ploughing was limited to the main paths. New stables, garages and a workshop were completed by 1954, the versatile park staff, as usual, did most of the work.

Fire has always been a serious hazard in the woodland. In a dry summer the bogs and streams disappear, leaving very limited water resources. After two fires in July 1956, the Commission decided to install two hydrants with a four-inch water line. The problem of ensuring a constant water supply to the hydrants was never completely resolved, and the situation was not markedly improved. The following year another fire occurred, but the staff's vigilance averted disaster. During particularly

Above left, the workshop is the building in the middle. (Castle)

Right, a fire hydrant in the woods (Castle)

The Tower Road parking lot 1996 (Castle)

Thomas Fripps, who had been an extremely successful park superintendent for thirty years, retired at the end of December 1959. He was presented with a chime clock by the Commission and a pair of gold cufflinks by the City of Halifax. Deputy Minister of Lands and Forests G. W. Creighton had a very high opinion of Tom Fripps' knowledge and skill and said that Mr. Fripps, although lacking in formal education on the subject, was capable of advising the City of Halifax on the care of its trees.

dry summers, when the danger of fire is considered severe, the Park is closed. In 1960, after a ten-day closure, it reopened when a rain storm offered relief.

As more and more people arrived at the Park in private vehicles, parking became less readily available. In 1957, two areas—one at Tower Road, the other near the beach—for twenty-seven cars were paved and, for a time, proved sufficient. Later, further paving at Tower Road continued regularly. Flower beds were eventually added around the parking areas.

Commercial tours (Parks Canada)

James (Jim) Nickerson beside one of his flower beds at Tower Road (Jim Nickerson)

His place was taken by James Nickerson, a long-time park employee, who moved into the lodge. Mayor Vaughan had suggested that Point Pleasant Park, like other city parks, should come under the supervision of the superintendent of Parks and Grounds, but the Commission was unwilling to give up control and felt strongly that a resident superintendent was essential.

From the Park's earliest days, horses were a common sight. They performed much of the heavy work, pulling wagons, carrying out forestry tasks and transporting employees. The carriage roads that encircled the perimeter and linked the forts were travelled by many smart barouches or more simple buggies drawn by high-stepping, well-groomed horses. The sheltered paths provided suitable routes for equestrian exercise. Away from busy cobbled streets, it was even a place for serious training of ponies destined to compete in trotting races. In winter, the trails were ideal for sleigh rides. In 1936, a local riding club requested a bridle path solely for horses, but the request was turned down.

In May 1946, the Commission made a rule that horses and horse-drawn vehicles were not permitted in the Park when it was most frequented, that is, between the hours of one in the afternoon and midnight from June to September, horses would be prohibited for public safety. Riders galloping recklessly three or more abreast, competing with one another, posed a danger to walkers and other riders, disrupted the peace, and

scared the wildlife; these had long been causes for
complaint. Frequent letters to the Commission and to
newspapers could not be ignored. In 1961, a new rule
was issued: No more horse racing in Point Pleasant Park!

In September 1951, the last workhorse owned by the
Park had to be put down because of ring bone. A
replacement was deemed unnecessary. Motorized
vehicles had taken over.

Commercial, horse-drawn tours of the Park took
place from time to time. After many walkers objected to
the damage to paths, the operator of surrey rides
equipped his horses with rubber shoes.

In 1968, a regular, mounted police patrol began and
proved "the best police protection ever." The horses
were stabled at the Park, and a police stableman was
employed there. The arrangement continued for more
than twenty years. Not only the mounted police patrol,
but the tall stableman who looked imposing as he rode
the trails, gave assistance and security to park users.

On January 18, 1988, the last two horses in the
Halifax Police Department's mounted division were
moved from their stable at the Park to the Bengal
Lancers' stables on Bell Road. The change would
reduce the cost of keeping the horses as the trained
farrier, necessary full-time at the park stables, could
now work elsewhere. The two horses, King and Babe,
continued some police duties but were also made

available to riders at the Bengal Lancers' Riding Academy.

A patrol in the Park did continue. Accommodation in the stable was requested for feeding and resting the horse. After only one mounted patrol remained and was seen less frequently in the Park, the Commission decided that "to maintain stables for a horse to have its lunch was no longer practical." The place was to be cleaned out and painted to remove "the horse odours that are prevalent throughout the building." The patrol officer, however, was extremely welcome in the Park and should feel free to make use of the facilities of the park building.

Occasionally, the question of allowing automobiles on the main paths has recurred, either for private vehicles or bus tours. After lengthy discussion, the disadvantages have always been judged to outweigh the merits of giving people who are unable to walk the chance to view the scenery and monuments. Non-motorized bicycles have always been permitted but, beginning in 1951, were banned on weekends and holidays, when the Park is especially busy. However, snowmobiles were not banned until February 1968.

In April 1964, the Department of National Defence decided that the park lands were no longer necessary to safeguard the region. The new authority would be the Department

Park crest, 1964 (P. P. P. Records)

Later editions of park brochure showing the new crest (P. P. P. Records)

of Northern Affairs and Natural Resources. The transfer was approved by the Commission, which would continue to operate in accordance with the 1873 lease. The superintendent of the Department of Northern Affairs, H. Johnson, remarked to the Point Pleasant Park Commission, "There are more historic structures per square foot in Point Pleasant Park than in any other site in Halifax," but just if the whole Park were declared a National Historic Site would his department wish to change the lease. To date, only the immediate area of the Martello Tower had been so designated.

The park crest, designed by Forbes Thrasher, was also produced in 1964. The wavy blue and white bands represent the waters of Halifax Harbour and the Northwest Arm, and the triangular green

projection the Park itself. The mural crown with mayflowers identifies with the City of Halifax.

The first descriptive brochure of the Park was printed during the same year. The white cover is embellished with the new park crest. Inside is a one-page description of the Park and some of its amenities, followed by a double-page map [reproduced inside front cover]. Colour photographs with captions and a page of interesting facts complete the booklet. For instance, the guided walk on the Nature Trail, established by the Nova Scotia Museum, was set up in 1962 and proved very popular. Unfortunately, vandalism and damage to the signs ended the trail's use, although it had been redone more than once. Simpler editions of the brochure came later.

In the summer of 1966, the swamp at the Tower Road entrance

The wall (Sonny Boutilier and Courtesy of The Halifax Herald Ltd.)

Building the wall, Sonny Boutilier and Hap Sawler (Sonny Boutilier and Courtesy of The Halifax Herald Ltd.)

to the Park was drained and the area landscaped.

On June 15, 1967, the Martello Tower was opened to the public, furbished with guides for the three summer months who were paid by the Department of Northern Affairs and National Resources.

The June 23, 1972, minutes of the Park Commission note that seven years earlier, work had commenced to enclose the park with a stone wall. Now it was complete. Built entirely by park staff, the cost had been kept to a minimum. Had it been contracted out, the cost would have been in the order of sixteen hundred dollars per one hundred feet.

In 1971, the newly appointed permanent director, Robert Kanigsberg, QC, suggested placing bird feeders in certain areas to supply food during the winter. Eventually, more were added, and these are kept filled year-round by park users.

Spring of 1976 brought tragedy to the shore of Point Pleasant. On Sunday, March 20, Ann Tulloch entered the Park around five-thirty in the afternoon to walk her two dogs. As she reached the anchor monument she saw about a hundred feet from shore a rowboat overturned and two men in the water clinging to it.

Ann, a non-swimmer, called out, "Do you think you could swim ashore if I walked out to meet you?" It did not seem too far for that.

One of them shouted back, "No! We'll stay with the boat." It seemed that one could not swim, and the other was trying to tow the boat ashore.

Ann yelled, "I'll go for help." She tore off her coat, and ran back to the parking lot. Unfortunately, she met no one on the way. However, a couple sat in a parked car. She

Above, Ann Tulloch Patrick (Ann Tulloch Patrick)

Above right, emergency telephones are at hand along the shore. (Castle)

hurriedly explained the situation and suggested that if they could find more people they might make a human chain out into the water. The man called the police. The woman headed quickly along the shore while Ann tried to find more helpers.

A police car arrived promptly. A young policeman considered swimming out to help, but by then the wind and currents had carried the men over a hundred yards offshore. The first rescue boats could not approach the men, now both face down in the water, as it was too shallow for their hulls. By the time a suitable boat reached the scene the men had been in the frigid water far too long, and it was

too late to save Ernest Guptill and John Vickery. The calamity revealed the weaknesses in the inner harbour rescue service. During the summer months a safety patrol kept watch in the Northwest Arm. Since this service ended in 1988, a police boat is on call. As a direct result of the deaths, emergency telephones were installed where they were considered most useful.

In the spring of 1989, the appearance of the park staff changed. The men had always worn their own work clothes, but for easier identification as well as neatness, they acquired dark blue uniforms. On their green caps was the park crest.

Security in the Park has also changed. Ports Canada officials had been worried by a sharp increase in thefts from container cars. By 1989, one major company had threatened to take their ships elsewhere. After discussions with the Park Commission, they agreed that a gate should

be placed at the entrance to the lower parking lot bordering on port lands, and that it should be closed at eleven o'clock each night, thus preventing cars easy access. This measure helped, but a few years later, the road leading from the city along the piers—a popular drive or run to the lower entrance—was closed completely.

In 1991, two uniformed special constables were employed to patrol the Park for the summer only. They went on foot or in the park truck. In recent years, the service has been extended to year-round, and the constables travel in a special vehicle. Also in 1991, the Venture Programme began, with young people patrolling on bicycles for summer park policing, which proved effective.

Spring 1995 marked the end of the services of the park restaurant. The original tearoom had proved successful. The building was supplied by the Commission, but the

Left, the park staff 1991: (rear, right to left) Edgar (Sonny) Boutilier, Larry Heighton, Steve Kidston, Gerald Bond, (front, right to left) Harold Briand, Gerald Gallant, David Large, Richard Bernard (Art Sampson)

Below, small canteen (Castle)

Bottom, the park restaurant is now home to Shakespeare by the Sea. (Castle)

facility was privately run. It was advertised for tender, and by 1940 the lease lasted three years. In 1948, two canteens with toilet facilities were planned, as it was decided most people wanted only ice cream and soft drinks. In 1949, the large canteen was finished, ready for lease. The small one stood near the beach. In 1967, after permanent water facilities were installed, the main building became more of a restaurant and stayed open year-round. In February 1969 it burned down. By August of the same year, a new, larger building was completed. It had both restaurant and canteen facilities. It was initially profitable, but by 1995, with fewer people using the beach and spend-ing the day at the Park, business dropped off. The small canteen at the beach was still busy, but the Commission decided to close the restaurant. In 1996, Shakespeare by the Sea used part of the building for

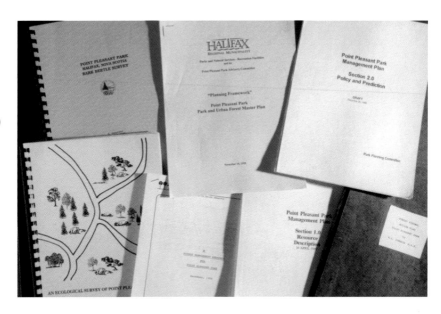

Park management plans (Castle)

storage, and it subsequently became the company's headquarters.

Forest management has always been a great concern for park commissioners and staff, who have never been completely expert in the matter. They have sought advice from the Department of Lands and Forests and other sources. A Forest Management Strategy for Point Pleasant Park by LaHave Forestry Consultants Ltd. was completed in 1984. For various reasons, lack of funds and manpower among them, the strategy was not seriously carried out. In 1989, a Forest Renewal Action Plan by forestry consultant W. L. Johnson, RPF, was about to be put into action by the Commission, but protests from different groups led to its abandonment. In 1990, a large Technical Advisory Committee was formed to make a plan for park management. An Ecological Survey was made by three members of Marbicon Inc., and Maritime Testing Limited in 1991. In June of that same year, the committee dissolved, and a smaller one, the Park Planning Committee, chaired by David Mann, QC, was later appointed. After a considerable amount of research and consultation, a complete plan was finished in 1995.

In 1991, a proposal was made that the Park be declared a Municipal Heritage Site. After much discussion, the Commission decided to delay such a move until the new management plan was completed, in case of necessary changes in the Park.

Not only the roads and forest require maintenance. The shoreline in certain areas of the Park is subject to erosion by the sea. Point Pleasant Battery has been badly affected. The nearby headland, where the war memorial once stood, has been considerably undermined. In 1991, shoreline protection work was carried out to prevent further damage to the area.

Walking dogs is one of the most popular park activities. Formerly, disciplined pets were allowed to run free at any time, causing some objections. Recently, in February 1994, a new rule was created:

No dogs on the Shore Road after ten in the morning year-round.

Annual park events include various sponsored walks and runs, orienteering meets and cross-country races for school groups, barbecues, picnics and many sponsored events for different causes. The Run for Light, held after dark to give blind and sighted runners the same advantage, appeals to the imagination. It was decided that large bicycle rides, such as the Manulife Ride for Heart, be discontinued because of the danger they posed to other park users. The Polar Bear Swim at Black Rock Beach on New Year's morning attracts more swimmers and spectators each year. Theatre in the Park is an increasingly popular summer attraction, with performances from Shakespeare by the Sea and the Shambhala Middle School.

When considering the progress of the Park, tribute must be paid to

the superintendents and park staff. Their versatility has been remarkable. They have acted as foresters, gardeners, stone masons, plumbers, mechanics, road builders. Indeed, the amount of work that has been contracted out is negligible. Throughout the Park's history, they have proved worthy caretakers. Former Commission Chairman Frank Bennett commented on this efficiency. The shed behind the workshop, a building thirty feet long, twenty feet wide and fifteen feet high with a gallery, was built entirely by the men, including the cement work. The total cost was twenty-two hundred dollars. "With that strength of workforce," he said, "we could do anything."

There have been seven superintendents, all with certain aptitudes and successes. Since Sir William Young, there have been many Commission chairmen. Citizens from many walks of life have served as park commissioners with dedication and love of the Park. During its 133 years, "The Park," as it is affectionately known to its countless users as if no other exists, has added immensely to their health and well-being.

Left, men who contributed greatly to the Park. Left to right, Superintendent Art Sampson, former Superintendent Loring (Hap) Sawler and foreman Edgar (Sonny) Boutilier (Castle)

Right, special cake at the 1993 staff Christmas party (park staff)

15
The Park Regulars

The sight of happy, active and generally well-behaved dogs is one of the pleasures, although perhaps not for everyone, of a walk in the Park. The different breeds exhibit their traits. The pointer stands perfectly still, nose extended towards the squirrel or bird. The collie encircles, trying to form a herd. The beagle runs, nose to the ground, picking up a scent. The aim of others is just to be friendly and appealing. Most are known by name to the regular human walkers.

"Good morning, Trix."

"Hello, Casey."

"Come and get your treat, Charlotte," to one who needs no second invitation.

"Where's your ball, Cinder?" and the ball is offered eagerly.

The individual dog's health and wellbeing is discussed. Bailey enjoyed the sail and a good swim at the weekend. Presumably his family did too, but that did not come into the conversation.

Food likes and dislikes, new helpful vitamins and herbal remedies are all discussed in connection with the pets. When such treatments have been found effective, humans have sometimes tried them, often with favourable results. It is, however, undoubtedly the exercise, fresh air and companionship that are of more benefit to the dogs and their owners than any medications.

Buddy probably enjoyed walking in the Park.

MAX

LOTTIE

MOLLIE

MADDY

SUGUS

CEILIDH

SUSIE

CASEY

DILLY

GRACE

OREO

CINDER

ZOE

NINJA

BAILEY

HAMLET

GOING FOR A SWIM

HECTOR

BEATRIX

GUS

MABEL

AMBER

SCHILLER

MONTROSE

DUDLEY

GINGER

DAISY

ABOU

SCOOTER

ROXY

BEULAH

HAGGIS & SNUG

TANGO & DUDEK

CASH

MILO

CHASE

COCO

PUCK

WINK

ABIGAIL

CHELSEA

POINT PLEASANT
PARK
INCORPORATED 1866

SHADOW

CHARLOTTE

MONTY

CHIN

Sources

Institutions and Printed Matter

Public Archives of Nova Scotia (We are especially obliged to Gary Schutlak for his knowledge and helpfulness.)

Province House Library

Point Pleasant Park Commission minutes and reports

City Hall records (V. Carmichael and many staff members)

Newspapers

Halifax Citadel (We wish to thank Ron Macdonald.)

Maritime Command Museum (our thanks to Marilyn Gurney)

Cambridge Military Library (Jean Howell)

Nova Scotia Museum (our gratitude to Scott Robson)

Roger Sarty, Senior Historian, Department of National Defence

The Trustees of the National Museums of Scotland

Sketches and Traditions of the Northwest Arm, J.W. Regan

Nova Scotia Historical Society papers, "Memoir of Lieutenant Governor Michael Francklyn," James Macdonald

Glimpses of Halifax, Phyllis Blakeney

Halifax, Warden of the North, Thomas H. Raddall

History of Halifax City, Dr. T. B. Atkins

The Evolution of the Halifax Fortress, 1749–1928, Harry Piers

Lord Dalhousie's Journals, edited by Marjorie Whitelaw

Encyclopedia Canadiana

Everyman's Encyclopedia

Encyclopedia Britannica

The Halifax Herald Limited (The management has been generous.)

Spring Garden Road Memorial Library Reference Department

Individuals

Muriel (Fripps) Griswold
Grace (Neate) Molineux
Carol Ann Janc
G. W. I. Creighton
H. David MacKeen
James Nickerson, Jr.
Ann Tulloch Patrick
Janet Piers
Anthony Lugar
Arthur Sampson
Lorne Sawler
Edgar Boutilier
G. Frank Bennett
Elliott Spafford
Eric Melvin
Judith Tulloch
Ronald Grantham

Judith Moreira
Richard Bernard
Gerald Bond
Kay MacIntosh
James Bennett
Debbie Reid
Fern Macdonald, New Glasgow Library
Rachel Yule
Peter Herschorn
Gareth Harding
James Clark
Sonia and Basil Grogono
Sydney Dumaresq
Brian Cuthbertson
Ruth Kimmins
Robert Weld
Shakespeare by the Sea
Shambhala Middle School

To everyone who lent a photograph or who contributed an idea or an anecdote, we wish to express our warm gratitude.